Corporate Acquisitions and Mergers in Bulgaria

AF897288

Corporate Acquisitions and Mergers in Bulgaria

Second Edition

Diana Dimova
Nina Tsifudina
Stiliyana Ivanova
Georgi Georgiev
Simeon Vachev
Denitsa Kuzeva
Kamen Chanov
Tsvetinka Andreeva

Kinstellar

This book was originally published as a chapter in Corporate Acquisitions and Mergers.

General Editor: Peter Begg

Wolters Kluwer

Published by:
Kluwer Law International B.V.
PO Box 316
2400 AH Alphen aan den Rijn
The Netherlands
E-mail: international-sales@wolterskluwer.com
Website: lrus.wolterskluwer.com

Sold and distributed in North, Central and South America by:
Wolters Kluwer Legal & Regulatory U.S.
7201 McKinney Circle
Frederick, MD 21704
United States of America
Email: customer.service@wolterskluwer.com

Sold and distributed in all other countries by:
Air Business Subscriptions
Rockwood House
Haywards Heath
West Sussex
RH16 3DH
United Kingdom
Email: international-customerservice@wolterskluwer.com

DISCLAIMER: The material in this volume is in the nature of general comment only. It is not offered as advice on any particular matter and should not be taken as such. The editor and the contributing authors expressly disclaim all liability to any person with regard to anything done or omitted to be done, and with respect to the consequences of anything done or omitted to be done wholly or partly in reliance upon the whole or any part of the contents of this volume. No reader should act or refrain from acting on the basis of any matter contained in this volume without first obtaining professional advice regarding the particular facts and circumstances at issue. Any and all opinions expressed herein are those of the particular author and are not necessarily those of the editor or publisher of this volume.

Printed on acid-free paper

ISBN 978-94-035-0974-7

e-Book: ISBN 978-94-035-1013-2
web-PDF: ISBN 978-94-035-1061-3

This title is available on www.kluwerlawonline.com

© 2019, Kluwer Law International BV, The Netherlands

All rights reserved. No part of this publication may be reproduced, stored in a retrieval system, or transmitted in any form or by any means, electronic, mechanical, photocopying, recording, or otherwise, without the prior written permission of the publisher.

Permission to use this content must be obtained from the copyright owner. More information can be found at: lrus.wolterskluwer.com/policies/permissions-reprints-and-licensing

Printed in the United Kingdom.

KINSTELLAR

Kinstellar is a leading independent law firm in Emerging Europe, Turkey and Central Asia, with offices in Almaty (Kazakhstan), Belgrade (Serbia), Bratislava (Slovakia), Bucharest (Romania), Budapest (Hungary), Istanbul (Turkey), Prague (the Czech Republic), Sofia (Bulgaria), Kyiv (Ukraine) and Tashkent (Uzbekistan).

Operating as a single, fully integrated firm, Kinstellar delivers consistent, high-quality services across all jurisdictions in an integrated and seamless style. We are particularly well suited to servicing complex transactions and advisory requirements spanning several jurisdictions. With offices in ten jurisdictions and over 140 local and international lawyers, we deliver consistent, joined-up legal advice and assistance across diverse regional markets.

Our clients include leading international and regional corporations, banks and other financial institutions, state bodies, multilateral institutions, and international law firms that require top-quality legal counsel in our jurisdictions. We handle the most important and complex assignments for clients across diverse industries and business sectors.

Kinstellar covers all aspects of domestic and international law, including Banking, Finance and Capital Markets, Competition and State Aid, Compliance, Risk and Sensitive Investigations, Dispute Resolution, Employment and Labour Law, Energy, Infrastructure and Projects, Intellectual Property, Life Sciences and Healthcare, M&A and Corporate, NPL's and Distressed Assets, Private Equity, Real Estate, Restructuring and Insolvency, Tax, Telecoms, Media and Technology.

Authors

This handbook was drafted by Stiliyana Ivanova (*Associate*), Denitsa Kuzeva (*Junior Associate*), Georgi Georgiev (*Junior Associate*), Kamen Chanov (*Junior Associate*), Simeon Vachev (*Junior Associate*) and Tsvetinka Andreeva (*Trainee Lawyer*).

The chapter has been reviewed and coordinated by Diana Dimova, *Managing Partner* of the Sofia office and Nina Tsifudina, *Managing Associate* Corporate/M&A.

Diana Dimova is a managing partner, the head of the M&A/Corporate practice in Sofia, and the firm-wide head of the Banking & Finance sector. She has over fifteen years of post-qualification experience. Diana advises corporations and financial institutions on a wide range of corporate and M&A matters, including the acquisition of private and listed companies, tender sales processes, restructuring and corporate governance. She has advised numerous international companies on their market entry and, subsequently, on the entire spectrum of ongoing corporate matters, including implementation of changes to their capital or corporate structures. Diana speaks Bulgarian and English.

Tel.: +359 2 9048 331
E-mail: diana.dimova@kinstellar.com

Nina Tsifudina is a managing associate in the M&A/Corporate and Employmer and Labour Law practices of the Sofia office. She has over ten years of pos qualification experience. She has advised both local and international clients on wide range of finance as well as corporate matters including assistance in enterin the Bulgarian market, M&A, restructuring and liquidations. Nina speal Bulgarian and English.

Tel.: +359 2 9048 341
E-mail: nina.tsifudina@kinstellar.com

Stiliyana Ivanova is an associate in the M&A/Corporate, Data Protection and Dat Privacy practice of the Sofia Office. She has assisted in the process of advising bot local and international clients with regards to a vast range of corporate and M& matters including establishment of their businesses in Bulgaria, corporat changes, day-to-day business activities and corporate governance. Stiliyana speal Bulgarian, English and Russian.

Tel.: +359 2 9048 342
E-mail: stiliyana.ivanova@kinstellar.com

Denitza Kuzeva is a junior associate. She focuses on employment, corporat banking and finance. She has previous experience in litigation. As a part of th Employment and Corporate practices, Denitsa assists domestic and internation clients with general corporate matters as well as various employment issues such compliance of employment agreements with Bulgarian legislation, dismissal internal rules and procedures. In the Banking and Finance practice, she focus on drafting of security documents, handling CPs collection and bankin regulations. Denitsa speaks Bulgarian, English and Russian.

Tel.: +359 2 9048 344
E-mail: denitsa.kuzeva@kinstellar.com

Georgi Georgiev is a junior associate. He focuses on corporate, energy, litigatic and compliance. Georgi is also a member of our extended dawn raids assistanc team. He has assisted clients in antitrust-related litigation before the Suprem Administrative Court and in ensuing out-of-court settlements. He also regular works on internal investigations and compliance audits. Georgi speaks Bulgaria and English.

Tel.: +359 2 9048 372
E-mail: georgi.georgiev@kinstellar.com

Kamen Chanov is a junior associate. He focuses on technology and competitic law and has valuable experience advising on compliance with European Unic and Bulgarian data protection legislation as well as working on antitrust an merger proceedings before the Bulgarian competition authority and the Supren Administrative Court. Before joining Kinstellar he worked at the Council of tl European Union in Brussels and at the Embassy of the Republic of Bulgaria i The Hague. Kamen speaks Bulgarian, English and French.

Tel.: +359 2 9048 358
E-mail: kamen.chanov@kinstellar.com

Simeon Vachev is a junior associate in the Real Estate, Corporate and M&A practices of the Sofia office. He has over three years of experience, advising both local and international companies on corner-stone real estate and banking projects in Bulgaria and the region. He has participated in negotiations and structuring of complex lease agreements, drafting and securitisation of credit facilities agreements as well as legal research and day-to-day business activities. Simeon speaks Bulgarian, English and Spanish.

Tel.: +359 2 9048 384
E-mail: simeon.vachev@kinstellar.com

Tsvetinka Andreeva is a trainee lawyer. She focuses on intellectual property, competition and information technology law. She has previous experience in protection of industrial property as well as litigation. She assists clients with various legal issues such as data protection, technology transfer, cybersecurity and consumer protection. Tsvetinka speaks Bulgarian, English and German.

Tel.: +359 2 9048 382
E-mail: tsvetinka.andreeva@kinstellar.com

Kinstellar, s.r.o., a.k./Branch Sofia/Ševčík

Infinity Tower, 14th floor

69 Bulgaria Blvd.

1404 Sofia, Bulgaria

Tel.: (359 2) 9048 300

Fax: (359 2) 9048 302
E-mail: diana.dimova@kinstellar.com Website: www.kinstellar.com

DISCLAIMER

This document does not purport to contain a comprehensive summary of all the legal risks and issues in the legal areas it covers. It is to be used for information only and cannot be relied upon as legal advice. No legal or business decision should be based solely on this document.

Contents

LEGAL, ECONOMIC, POLITICAL AND CULTURAL ASPECTS

General Comments on the Country Profile

Geographic Location

[01] Bulgaria is located in the south-east of Europe as part of the Balkan Peninsula – a region steeped in history, situated between three continents: Europe, Asia and Africa.

[02] Bulgaria is bordered by the Black Sea to the east, Romania to the north, Serbia and Macedonia to the west and Greece and Turkey to the south. The Danube River marks the border with Romania. The capital and largest city is Sofia, which is the fifteenth largest city in the European Union (EU) by population.

[03] The territory of Bulgaria occupies approximately 111 000 square kilometres, which ranks it sixteenth in size in Europe[1] and eleventh in the EU.

[04] Located at the heart of the Balkans, Bulgaria is a strategic logistics hub. Five pan-European corridors[2] pass through its territory. The country has two main seaports that provide access to the Black Sea. Numerous ports are situated along the Danube River. Bulgaria participates in the Transport Corridor Europe-Caucasus-Asia ('*TRACECA*') transport programme.

[05] Due to its geography, Bulgaria has good conditions for tourism. The well-developed summer resorts and small villages, which enjoy access to thermal mineral springs, welcome tourists during the summer, while the beautiful mountainous areas attract hikers and skiers/snowboarders all year long.

Population and Population Growth

[06] The population of Bulgaria is 7 050 034,[3] which represents 1.4% of the population of the EU. The current demographic situation in the country is characterised by a continuing decrease in the population number,[4] an ageing population and relatively high levels of mortality. In 2014 there was a slight decrease in crude birth rate and in life expectancy at birth compared with 2016.

[07] Statistical information for 2017 shows that Bulgaria has a negative population growth of 0.7%.

---

[1] Including countries that are also considered part of Asia, whose territories are ranked by the area of their European parts only – e.g., Russia, Kazakhstan.

[2] Pan-European Corridors – IV, VII, VII, XI and X.

[3] According to official statistics of the Bulgarian National Statistical Institute of Bulgaria as of 31 Dec. 2017.

[4] The population decreased in 2017, compared to 2016, by 51 825479.

[08] Most of the population lives in the cities. The number of registered inhabi ants of Sofia is 1 266 295, but many people work in the capital and travel fro other parts of the country on a daily basis.

Language

[09] The official language is Bulgarian.

[10] English is very widely spoken, especially in big cities and tourist areas. Th younger generation also speaks other foreign languages – German, Spanis French, etc., while Russian is popular among the older population.

Natural Resources

[11] Bulgaria has bauxite, copper, lead, zinc, coal, timber and other natur resources.

There are areas with arable land that have good agricultural potential. While th average price per decare has increased steadily since 2010, the gross value of agr cultural produce in 2017 decreased by 1.7% compared to 2016.

The country is rich in mineral waters.

The potential for photovoltaic energy production is good, and it is also well ut lised, as the country's support scheme for renewable energy projects was quite ge erous in the past.

Currency

[12] The national currency is Bulgarian lev (pl. 'leva'). The Bulgarian lev is a leg tender and must be accepted as payment at full face value.

[13] After legislative amendments in 1996, the parties to a contract can free choose foreign currency as consideration for their contract. This is possible even both parties to a contract are Bulgarian individuals or entities. Recently, tl Supreme Court of Cassation had the opportunity to rule that obligations for pa ment in foreign currency cannot be awarded in leva and payment should be mac in the agreed currency.[5]

[14] As of 1 July 1997, Bulgaria introduced a currency board by passing a speci law, which remains in force today. Currently, the Bulgarian national curren (BGN) is fixed to the official currency of the Eurozone (EUR). As noted above, tl exchange rate is fixed at BGN1.95583/EUR1. In July 2018, Bulgaria received tl Eurogroup's nod of approval to start official preparations to join the Eurozone. preliminary step in that direction is acceding to the Exchange Rate Mechanis (also known as the 'ERM-II'). Set on joining the ERM-II and the EU's bankir union, in September the Bulgarian Council of Ministers adopted an action pl containing detailed measures to be implemented by no later than July 2019.

[5] There might be some exceptions to this rule in the applicable legislative acts.

Employment Cost and Availability of Labour

[15] The two main components that form employment costs are: (i) the employee's salary; and (ii) taxes and social security contributions.

[16] The salary is freely negotiated, but the law prescribes a statutory minimum amount, which is determined by the Council of Ministers. The minimum salary is usually determined once per calendar year. As of January 2018, the statutory minimum amount is BGN510 (approximately EUR260) for a full-time job or BGN3.07 (approximately EUR1.57) per working hour.[6]

[17] The taxes and social security contributions are split between the employer and the employee. This includes social security contributions on behalf of the employee (approximately 13.8% of the gross salary), social security contributions on behalf of the employer (approximately 18.92% of the gross salary). Income tax is a flat rate of 10%.

[18] Bulgaria is one of the two countries in the EU with the lowest average hourly labour cost.[7]

[19] For the third quarter of 2018, the unemployment rate was 5%.[8]

[20] The literacy rate in Bulgaria is 98.4%,[9] which is generally high. It is common for young people to pursue higher education in Bulgaria.

[21] The IT and manufacturing sectors are developing rapidly, and many people are employed in these sectors. There are regions with high unemployment that enjoy beneficial treatment from the state. People in those areas are willing to work for salaries which are below the average. This makes such places attractive for manufacturing and production facilities.

Infrastructure

[22] Bulgaria has 19 861 kilometres of roads, of which 734 kilometres are motorways.[10] A motorway connects the capital (Sofia) with the city of Bourgas, which is located by the Black Sea. Some roads require maintenance and new investment. The government has expressed interest in improving the road network across the country. Among the major projects are further construction of the Struma (part of the Pan-European Corridor IV and also part of E79) and the Hemus (A2) motorways.

[6] As of January 2019, the minimum salary will become BGN 560 (approximately EUR280) for a full-time job or BGN 3.33 (approximately EUR1.71) per working hour.

[7] According to Eurostat news release No. 60 dated 9 Apr. 2018: *Labour costs in the EU*.

[8] According to official statistics of the National Statistical Institute of Bulgaria, dated 14 Nov. 2018.

[9] According to the country profile of Bulgaria, available on the Central Intelligence Agency (CIA) World Factbook website.

[10] According to official statistics of the Bulgarian National Statistical Institute of Bulgaria as of 31 Dec. 2017.

[23] The total length of railroads in Bulgaria is 4 030 kilometres. Improvement of the conditions for railroad transportation is one of the government's top priorities for the sector.

[24] Bulgaria has four major international airports, which are situated in Sofia, Varna, Plovdiv and Bourgas. The country's leading international airport is located in the capital – Sofia. The operation of the airport is currently the subject of a concession procedure.

Government and Political System

Political Stability

[25] Bulgaria is organised as a democratic parliamentary republic. The Prime Minister is the head of government, while the President exercises the functions of head of state.

[26] The legislative power is vested in the parliament, while the executive power is performed by the government. The judiciary system is independent of the executive and legislative systems.

[27] Bulgaria has a multiparty system. In 2013 there were snap elections for members of parliament, but currently the parliament is stable. Currently five parties are represented in the parliament, the three leading ones being – CEDB[11] (37.6%) BSP[12] (31.6%) and United Patriots[13] (10.8%).

[28] Bulgaria is generally a politically stable country that welcomes and encourages foreign investments.

Entrepreneurship Environment

[29] During the past few years there has been a visible trend towards an improvement in the entrepreneurial environment and an increase in start-up initiatives especially in the IT sector. Start-up projects have become more and more attractive to investors. In October 2016, Sofia was listed by *Forbes* magazine among the top ten destinations for business start-ups.[14] Some start-up accelerators, such as Eleven, LAUNCHub and others (operating through the JEREMIE Programme of the European Investment Fund), are active in Bulgaria, as well as later-stage investors such as Neveq and BlackPeak Capital.

[30] In December 2015, a new state-owned company named Sofia Tech Park started operations. The main goal of the company is to boost the development of

[11] Citizens for European Development of Bulgaria (in Bulgarian: '*Граждани за европейско развитие България – ГЕРБ*').

[12] Bulgarian Socialist Party (in Bulgarian: '*Българска социалистическа партия – БСП*').

[13] United Patriots (in Bulgarian: '*Обединени патриоти*').

[14] https://www.forbes.com/sites/amyguttman/2015/11/29/top-10-cities-in-the-world-to-launch-your-startup-some-may-surprise-you/#6ddf3f297e57.

research, innovation and technological capabilities of Bulgaria through implementing various projects. For this purpose, Sofia Tech will collaborate with private and public institutions in order to create and manage a unique environment for innovation, build and implement educational programmes and provide support for the commercialisation of new technologies, products and services.

Legal System

[31] Bulgaria has a civil law legal system. Legislation is influenced by the French, Italian and German legal systems. Bulgaria has not yet codified its substantive civil law in a single legislative act – a civil code. However, the other branches of law are systematically being codified (Administrative Procedure Code, Criminal Code, etc.)

[32] Business people and legal practitioners who are used to working in civil law jurisdictions will feel at ease with the structure of commercial law in Bulgaria. However, the legal system would seem quite different to business people and legal practitioners accustomed to a common law environment.

[33] Generally, laws are enforced relatively efficiently by public authorities, but court proceedings can take a significant amount of time before reaching a final resolution. Bulgaria has a three-tiered court system, but the third tier is not compulsory and only a limited number of cases go there.

[34] Bulgaria ranks fortieth out of 190 economies in terms of the enforcing contracts indicator.[15]

[35] Acquisition targets are easily identified. Investors can gain information about targets through law firms, professional consultants or by directly contacting the responsible authorities – the privatisation agency, InvestBulgaria Agency and others.

Current Economic Aspects

Growth Rate of Economy

[36] Bulgaria had a gross domestic product (GDP) growth rate of 3.0% in the third quarter of 2018 compared to the same period in 2017.[16] The annual growth rate is expected to increase slightly in 2019 to 3.7%.[17]

[15] According to data from the World Bank's 'Doing Business' project; the data is current as of October 2018.

[16] According to official statistics of the National Statistical Institute of Bulgaria.

[17] According to data published on the website of the Bulgarian Ministry of Finance: http://www.minfin.bg/bg/866.

[37] As of December 2018, the annual average inflation[18] is expected to reac 2.7%. Inflation is expected to rise to 3% in 2019 and is forecasted to slow down b the end of the year.

[38] The prognosis of the public budget balance for 2018 is 4.4% of GDP and projected to decrease to 4.2% of GDP in 2019.

M&A Trends

[39] In 2017, the trend was for an increase in M&A transactions. According t 'Emerging Europe: M&A Report 2017/18',[19] there were 82 M&A deals closed i 2017 with a total deal value of approximately EUR1.45 bn. The main areas fc M&A transactions were real estate and construction, telecoms & IT, manufacturin finance & insurance and wholesale & retail trade.

[40] As the Bulgarian economy is on upward trend, we expect other significar local M&A transactions, especially in sectors such as real estate, telecoms & I manufacturing, finance & insurance.

Main Industries

Key Industries

[41] The key industries in Bulgaria are:

(i) *Agriculture* – Bulgaria enjoys excellent natural conditions for developin the agriculture and forestry sectors. Cultivated agricultural land occupi over 5 m hectares, or 45.3% of the total territory of the country. The favou able climate, availability of agricultural land and long-standing traditio have resulted in well-developed plant varieties and animal breeds. Oth advantages are low labour costs and high schools and colleges offerin training in modern farming and animal breeding.[20]

(ii) *Energy* – Bulgaria has good photovoltaic potential and some wind pote tial. It generally produces sufficient electricity to satisfy its own needs whi exporting the excess capacity.[21]

(iii) *IT* – The development of the IT & software industry is part of the key pr orities of the government. The sector currently enjoys a stable growth

[18] According to official statistics of the Ministry of Finance.

[19] Available here: https://emerging-europe.com/news/emerging-europe-sees-surge-in-ma-deals/.

[20] According to the official statistics published on the website of the Ministry of Agriculture, Food a Forestry for December 2017, available here: http://www.mzh.government.bg/media/filer_publ 2018/11/15/ra_334-publicationbancik2017.pdf.

[21] According to the CIA World Factbook, Bulgaria exported 9.187 bn kWh in 2017: https://www.cia.g library/publications/the-world-factbook/fields/2234.html.

around 30% per year. Key advantages of the industry include the availability of a highly qualified workforce, competitive pricing, many talented young people majoring in IT and long-standing traditions.[22]

(iv) *BPO* – Bulgaria is a popular BPO destination mainly due to the availability of qualified personnel and low labour costs. Bulgaria is ranked fifteenth in the consultancy group's Global Services Location Index 2017, higher than any other nation in the same region.[23]

(v) *Pharma* – Bulgaria's location, its tradition of drug production and the quality of production makes it a good place for investments.

(vi) *Manufacturing* – Bulgaria offers qualified engineers, traditions and experience in this sector. Easy access to both the EU and Russian markets makes the country very attractive to foreign investors. Machine building and engineering are being expanded, especially for light electrical equipment. The automotive sector is booming as well, as demonstrated by the increasing volume of greenfield investments.[24]

(vii) *Telecom sector* – Bulgaria is one of the smallest telecom service markets in Central and Eastern Europe (CEE). In both the fixed and mobile segments, growth will be driven mainly by data services. Fixed broadband is expected to grow faster, helped by a national broadband plan aimed at expanding access in rural areas. Although Bulgaria has an e-skills strategy and implementation plan, a concept for the digital transformation of the industry and an e-government strategy, it continues to rank among the lowest performing EU Member States on the Digital Economy and Society Index.[25]

(viii) *Gold extraction* – Bulgaria has 40.3 tonnes of gold reserves and ranks forty-ninth in global rankings by gold reserves, according to data from the World Gold Council.[26]

Foreign Investments

[42] Bulgarian legislation provides for the national treatment of foreign investors.

[43] The legal regime for the acquisition of agricultural land is somewhat controversial, and there are still some restrictions in place. The following types of companies cannot acquire agricultural land:

(i) companies whose shareholders are directly or indirectly companies registered in a preferential tax treatment jurisdiction (tax haven);

[22] According to information from the private consultancy company – Invest Bulgaria, available here: http://www.investbulgaria.com/BulgarianSoftwareSector.php.

[23] The annual index monitors financial attractiveness, people skills and availability, among others.

[24] More information can be found in this brochure of the InvestBulgaria Agency: http://www.investbg.government.bg/files/useruploads/files/brochures2013/en/machine_building_en-2.pdf.

[25] More information can be found here: http://ec.europa.eu/information_society/newsroom/image/document/2018-20/bg-desi_2018-country-profile_eng_B43F6DD5-FDA8-134C-B36DA7214990F864_52215.pdf.

[26] World Official Gold Holdings, International Financial Statistics, February 2017.

(ii) companies whose shareholders are from a non-EU/European Economic Area (EEA) country with which Bulgaria does not have a bilateral treaty;
(iii) joint-stock companies that have emitted bearer shares.

[44] There is an exemption to the restrictions under (i) and (ii) above for public companies and real estate investment trusts.

[45] Individuals and legal entities that are willing to acquire agricultural land have to adhere to a residency requirement (five years of residence). Legal entities whose shareholders comply with the residency requirement are exempt from the restriction.

[46] Specific restrictions also apply to offshore companies/contractual partnerships that want to acquire ownership of land and forests from the State Forest Fund

[47] Bulgaria provides investment promotion measures under the Investment Promotion Act. Certified projects, among other measures, could benefit from:

(i) shortened terms for administrative procedures;
(ii) acquisition of title or other rights in rem without tender;
(iii) financial aid;
(iv) tax exemptions under the Corporate Income Tax Act (CITA).[27]

[48] Bulgaria has concluded many Bilateral Treaties for Mutual Protection and Encouragement of Investments. Bulgaria is also a party to the Energy Charter Treaty.

Role of the State in the Economy

[49] Foreign investments are allowed in all sectors of the economy. The state has a strong presence in the energy sector and owns Bulgarian Energy Holding (*BEH*). BEH is the owner of AEC Kozloduy EAD (nuclear power plant operator), Natsionala Elektricheska Kompania EAD (electricity public supplier), Elektroenergien Sistemen Operator EAD (electricity transmission system operator), Bulgargaz EAD (natural gas public supplier), Bulgartransgaz EAD (natural gas transmission system operator) and many others.

[50] The national postal service, Bulgarski Poshti EAD, and the national railway holding company, Holding Bulgarski Durjavni Jeleznitsi EAD, are also owned by the state.

Local M&A Deals

[51] According to M&A Barometer H1 2017 Central and Southeast Europe,[28] the Bulgarian market was dominated by inbound transactions – 48%, while domestic

[27] For more details, please see paras [222]–[255].

[28] Available here: https://www.ey.com/Publication/vwLUAssets/ey-csema-barometer-2017/$FILE/ey-csema-barometer-2017.pdf.

transactions represented 35% of closed deals. For this period, outbound transactions represented 17% of deals.

[52] The largest deal by volume closed in 2017 was the acquisition of United Bulgarian Bank and Interlease Leasing by KBC Group, with a deal value of approximately EUR610 m. Kinstellar's Sofia office advised on the buyer's side.

[53] Other significant transactions in 2017 include:

(i) the acquisition of the Bulgarian bottled water and distributor Devin AD by the family-owned company Spadel;
(ii) the acquisitions of four shopping centres, as follows:
   - Acquisition of Paradise Centre and Serdika Centre and Office by the South-African investor NEPI Rockcastle;
   - Acquisition of The Mall by the South-African company Hyprop Investment Limited;
   - Acquisition of the shopping centre Galleria in Burgas and Stara Zagora by the South-African fund MAS Real Estate;
(iii) the purchase of the automotive company Moto-Pfohe by the Japanese corporation Sumitomo.

[54] In 2017, deals in Bulgaria involved mainly strategic investors – 82%, while financial investors represented 18% of deals.

[55] According to information from *Capital* newspaper, as of October 2018, some of the more significant transactions for 2018 are:

(i) acquisition of the telecommunication company Telenor Bulgaria with a deal value above EUR800 m;
(ii) acquisition of the French bank Societe Generale Expressbank by the Bulgarian bank DSK, with a deal value of approximately EUR500 m;
(iii) acquisition of the office building Megapark with a deal value of around EUR100 m. Kinstellar's Sofia office advised on the buyer's side.

Cultural Aspects

Investments Climate

[56] Bulgaria is ranked fiftieth out of 190 in the World Bank's annual Ease of Doing Business Index 2018. Doing business in Bulgaria is facilitated by the fact that English is widely spoken, that the country offers a well-educated workforce at a competitive price, and that Bulgaria has strategic location. However, judicial, legislative and regulatory unpredictability continue to negatively affect the investment climate.

[57] Bulgaria is a relatively cheap place for doing business. Labour costs are not high and therefore Bulgaria is considered a good place to outsource services and business processes, especially for IT outsourcing. It is ranked fifteenth among fift five countries in the Global Services Location Index. Manufacturing compani find the country attractive because of: (i) the skilled employees; (ii) lower costs fc operating a factory (compared to other SEE countries); and (iii) Bulgaria's clos location to the western European market. There are a number of industrial zon offering attractive plots at competitive prices.

[58] Bulgaria has a higher level of bureaucracy compared to jurisdictions such Germany and the UK, and administrative procedures can sometimes be burde some. With regards to corruption, Bulgaria has been perceived to have made sig nificant strides in the years 2017 and 2018, although room for improvement is st considered to exist. The European Commission's overall conclusions in its repo on Bulgaria's progress under the Cooperation and Verification Mechanism fro 2018 have overall been positive. However, the judiciary system is still perceived b international businesses operating in Bulgaria to lack sufficient expedience an objectivity. With respect to the level of personal security awareness, it is advisable t maintain the same level as in other countries within the EU.

Exchange of Gifts

[59] In Bulgaria, exchanges of discrete gifts of marginal value between busine partners with established commercial relations are considered polite. The gift do not have to be expensive. If the guest is a foreigner, the gift may be a tradition souvenir, sweets or sometimes even a typical alcoholic beverage from the visitor country. These gifts are considered a sign of international cooperation and are us ally opened immediately.

[60] One should note that many medium-sized and large companies, especial those having an international background, have already introduced ant corruption policies regarding the exchange of gifts. Furthermore, giving gifts government officials or people working in the state administration is not consi ered a normal feature of day-to-day business and is therefore unadvisable.

[61] Bulgarians in general, like other people in Eastern Europe, are very hosp table.

Cultural Differences

[62] Business relationships are an important part of the Bulgarian business cu ture. Newcomers are usually treated very formally until there has been time to g to know them. After that, once a business relationship has been established, it usually a long-term one based on loyalty and trust.

[63] Bulgarians are family oriented. Certain events such as birthdays, funeral marriages and the relevant Orthodox celebrations are important to Bulgarians.

[64] One should be aware of the peculiarity of head shaking/nodding. In Bulgar most people use these gestures in the opposite way to the way in which they a used in western cultures. Very often, a shake of the head indicates affirmation (yes while nodding would mean rejection (no). Some young people who are aware of this distinction would reverse the gestures when speaking to foreigners. So one can never be absolutely sure what a person means by relying on the head gesture alone.

THE REGULATORY FRAMEWORK

Business Vehicles in Bulgaria

Forms of Business Vehicles

[65] The types of trade companies in Bulgaria and their legal status are regulated in the Bulgarian Commercial Act (*BCA*). Under the BCA there are five types of companies that can be set up in Bulgaria:

(i) general partnership (in Bulgarian: ***събирателно дружество***);
(ii) limited partnership (in Bulgarian: ***командитно дружество***);
(iii) limited liability company (*LLC*) (in Bulgarian: ***дружество с ограничена отговорност***);
(iv) joint-stock company (*JSC*) (in Bulgarian: ***акционерно дружество***);
(v) partnership limited by shares (in Bulgarian:an: ***командитно дружество с акции***).

[66] Other more recent forms of establishment introduced by European law are the European Company[29] and the European Economic Interests Grouping (EEIG).[30]

[67] Foreign legal entities can also register their branches in Bulgaria. A branch of a legal entity is usually registered for the purpose of smaller business initiatives and investments. The branch, however, is not a separate legal entity. The foreign legal entity becomes a party under the contracts signed by the branch. Thus, the foreign legal entity is directly liable for the obligations of its branch.

[68] The LLC and the JSC are the most common corporate structures used for undertaking commercial activity in Bulgaria. Both provide for the limited liability of the shareholders and can be set up as wholly owned companies. Both legal entities and individuals may become a shareholder in an LLC or a JSC. LLCs and JSCs can be engaged in practically all types of commercial activities not prohibited by Bulgarian law.

[69] From the compliance point of view, although LLCs and JSCs can be engaged in practically all types of commercial activities, certain types of businesses may be conducted only upon receipt of a special permission, registration or licence.

[29] The legal status of the European Company is regulated in Regulation (EC) No. 2157/2001 of 8 Oct. 2001 on the Statute for a European Company (SE).

[30] The legal status of the European Economic Interests Grouping is regulated in Regulation (EEC) No. 2137/85 of 25 Jul. 1985 on the European Economic Interest Grouping (EEIG).

[70] In addition, Bulgarian legislation places special requirements on companies in some areas, for example: the type of company that can be engaged in certain businesses (e.g., only JSCs can be licenced as banks or insurance companies), a minimum amount of the share capital (e.g., credit institutions), a certain educational level of the legal representatives, etc.

Registration Requirements

Registration with the Commercial Registry

[71] In order to come into legal existence, all five types of companies are registered at the Commercial Registry (*CR*) with the Bulgarian Registry Agency. The registration of the respective company takes one business day from the date of filing of the required documents.

[72] Once registered, the respective company obtains a unified identification number and is fully operational, including for tax purposes. From the date of registration, the CR maintains a separate file for each registered company. The file contains information on the current status of the company (e.g., company name, unified identification number (*in Bulgarian:* ***ЕИК***), name of the legal representative's, manner of representation, seat and registered office, scope of activity, amount of registered capital and paid-in capital, shareholder/s and name of the procurator/s (if any) and any pledges established over the shares or the going concern of the company).

[73] The *CR* keeps track of the submitted applications and documents, the corporate changes executed since the incorporation of the company and the announced acts, e.g., annual financial statements and articles of association of the company. The information is publicly available at: http://brra.bg/.

[74] Changes in the circumstances registered at the CR (such as, but not limited to changes in the share capital, legal representatives, seat and registered office, should be submitted for registration within seven days of the change or the adoption of the act/s subject to announcement. In most of the cases, registration at the *CR* only has a declarative effect regarding third parties.

VAT Registration with the National Revenue Agency

[75] A company, regardless of its form – LLC, JSC or other type of company should register for Value Added Tax (VAT) if its turnover exceeds BGN50 000 (approximately EUR25 500) for twelve consecutive months. It may also register voluntarily for VAT purposes at any time.

Registration with a State Authority

[76] A company operating in a regulated sector may be subject to registration with a special public registry following procedures specified in Bulgarian legislation. Such registration often requires compliance with certain requirements such as a minimum amount of share capital, educational level of the legal representatives or employee, average number of employees.

Reporting Requirements

Revealing of Information Before the CR

[77] Since 1 January 2014, a special piece of legislation – the Economic and Financial Relations with Companies Registered in Preferential Tax Treatment Jurisdictions, Parties Controlled by Them and Their Beneficial Owners Act (the *Offshore Act*) – has been in force in Bulgaria.

[78] The Offshore Act prohibits offshore companies and parties controlled by them from acquiring directly or indirectly share participations in Bulgarian companies engaged in certain economic sectors. The restricted list includes, among others: credit and payment institutions; insurance and pension companies; investment intermediaries and regulated markets; collective investment undertakings and alternative investment funds; mobile, TV and radio operator companies; publishers of periodicals; licensed energy undertakings (e.g., electricity traders, electricity generators operating power plants with installed capacity of more than 5 MW, end suppliers); companies operating renewable energy power plants (regardless of the installed capacity or the renewable energy source).

[79] The Offshore Act also prohibits offshore companies and parties controlled by them from participating directly or indirectly in public tenders, privatisations, concessions, acquisition of state or municipal properties, etc. The sanctions for non-compliance are severe – a transaction concluded in breach of the restrictions could be declared null and void. In some cases the target company's licence could be withdrawn.

[80] The Offshore Act provides certain exceptions to the above restrictions. Among others, if an offshore company or its related party intends to acquire an interest in a Bulgarian company engaged in a restricted sector, or to participate in a restricted procedure, the offshore company's beneficial owners (within the meaning of §2 of the Supplementary Provisions of the Act on the Measures against Money Laundering) should be disclosed from the outset. To that effect, the beneficial owners should be registered at the CR. The same obligation also applies to investors which: (i) already hold shares in Bulgarian companies falling within the scope of the act; and (ii) are somehow affiliated with offshore companies.

[81] In March 2018, a new Act on the Measures against Money Laundering (the *Anti-Money Laundering (AML) Act*) was adopted in order to transpose to Bulgarian legislation Directive (EU) 2015/849 on the prevention of the use of the financial system for the purposes of money laundering or terrorist financing.

[82] Ultimate beneficial owners are considered to be natural persons ultimately owning or controlling, directly or indirectly, a corporate or another legal entity. The definition applies also to natural persons on whose behalf the entity carries out a particular operation, transaction or activity.

[83] Particularly with respect to LLCs and JSCs, a natural person directly or indirectly owning at least 25% of the shareholding in that entity qualifies as its ultimate beneficial owner for the purposes of the AML Act.

[84] By 1 June 2019, all LLCs and JSCs established in Bulgaria must disclose the ultimate beneficial owners in the *CR*. With the exception of publically listed con panies (i.e., the shares of which are traded on regulated markets), the requiremer to disclose the ultimate beneficial owners applies not only to companies but also t economic enterprises (such as trusts, etc.) and non-profit organisations (such a foundations and associations).

Annual Closing of LLC and JSC

[85] By 31 March each year, both LLCs and JSCs registered in Bulgaria are oblige to prepare annual financial statements for the previous financial year, i.e., for th period ended 31 December of the previous calendar year. The company's annu financial statements are signed by the accountant (or the preparer) and by its mar aging director. The annual financial statements are comprised of the balance shee income statement, cash-flow statement, statement of changes in equity and accon panying notes. Companies falling within the criteria for mandatory financial aud also have to prepare an annual report on the activity.

[86] A JSC is subject to a mandatory financial audit, unless it falls within the scop of the definition of a 'microenterprise' under the Accountancy Act, i.e., if it mee or exceeds at least two of the following requirements: (i) a book value of assets BGN700 000 (approximately EUR357 928); (ii) annual net sales of BGN1.4 (approximately EUR700 000); and (iii) an average number of ten employees fo the year. An LLC should appoint auditors, if it falls within the scope of the defin tion of a 'small enterprise' and it meets or exceeds at least two of the followin requirements: (i) book value of the assets of BGN2, m (approximately EUR1 m); (i annual net sales of BGN4 m (approximately EUR2 045 306); and (iii) an averag number of 50 employees for the year.

[87] Following the preparation of the annual financial statements and their aud (if applicable), the sole shareholder or the general meeting of the shareholde approves the annual financial statements and the audit report by virtue of a res lution. By virtue of the same resolution the main corporate body may decide on th profit distribution, release the managing director/s from liability, etc.

Filing with the CR

[88] Annual financial statements, along with the auditors' report and the activi report (if applicable), should be announced with the CR under the company's fi and should also be filed with the National Statistical Institute. These documen should be submitted to the CR by 30 June of the year following the respectiv accounting year.

Regulated Activity Reporting

[89] If the activity of LLCs and JSCs is regulated, they may need to present annu financial statements or other information/documents for their activity covering certain period of time to the specialised state authorities.

Tax Return

[90] By 31 March each year, the LLC and JSC must file their annual tax return with the respective office of the National Revenue Agency together with an annual report on the activity (for companies preparing such) and must pay their corporate tax on the realised profits. Currently the corporate tax rate is 10%. Non-operating companies are not obliged to submit to the tax authorities their annual tax return if they have not performed activity (under the meaning of the Accountancy Act) for the respective tax period.

Declaring of Transactions Relating to Foreign Exchange

[91] For statistical purposes, Bulgarian legal entities should declare certain types of transactions to the Bulgarian National Bank within fifteen business days of their execution. These transactions are:

(i) direct investments abroad, regardless of the amount of the investment;
(ii) transactions between local and foreign persons involving incoming and outgoing loans exceeding BGN50 000 (approximately EUR25 500);
(iii) opening of bank accounts abroad, regardless of the amount of money transferred to the account.

International Payments and Transfers

[92] Depending on the amount, companies are required to report their receivables from and liabilities to foreign legal entities and individuals to the Bulgarian National Bank.

General Characteristics of an LLC

Basic Characteristics

[93] An LLC can be formed by one or more Bulgarian or foreign individuals and/or legal entities. The number of founders is not restricted. LLCs are liable for their obligations with all of the assets and property belonging to them. The shareholders in an LLC do not assume personal liability for the debts of the company.

[94] An LLC is incorporated for commercial activity. The basic economic function of an LLC is to conduct small- and medium-sized business. This is due to certain advantages of an LLC as compared to a JSC, for example, lower minimum amount of capital and simplified corporate governance.

Founding and Registration

[95] An LLC is established by fulfilment of three main steps, namely: (i) execution of articles of association, or incorporation deed in the case of a solely owned LLC; (ii) payment of the contributions of the shareholders at least in the amount of the legislative minimum; and (iii) registration at the CR.

[96] The articles of association or the incorporation deed are signed by the founders of the LLC in simple written form. The BCA provides for the minimum contents of the company's articles (e.g., name, seat and registered office, scope of activity, amount of the registered capital).

[97] Upon registration at the CR, the LLC comes into legal existence and becomes fully operational.

[98] Shareholders in LLCs are registered in the CR, while no such requirements apply to JSCs, except in the case of a solely owned JSC.

Registered Capital

[99] The registered capital of an LLC cannot be lower than BGN2 (approximately EUR1). It is composed of the shares of the shareholders, which cannot have a value lower than BGN1. The participation of shareholders can be unequal. One share can be held jointly by more than one person.

[100] If an LLC is registered with capital higher than the minimum amount, at least 70% of the capital should be paid-in. The remaining part of the amount should be paid-in within a term not longer than two years from the registration of the company.

[101] According to the BCA, two types of capital contributions are allowed:

(i) pecuniary (cash) contribution; and
(ii) in-kind contribution – an in-kind contribution executed in an LLC is subject to valuation by three experts appointed by the CR. The price of the shares that a person initially subscribes to in his/her/its name in the LLC should not exceed the expert valuation of the in-kind contribution, i.e., it can be equal or lower.

[102] Shares in an LLC are subject to transfer and inheritance. The transfer of shares from one shareholder to another in an LLC is simplified, while the transfer of shares from existing to new shareholders requires the approval of the shareholders' meeting.

[103] The BCA provides for the transfer of shares to be executed by virtue of a written agreement with notarisation of the signatures and the content of the agreement. The share transfer should then be registered at the CR.

Corporate Bodies

[104] The corporate bodies of an LLC are the general meeting of the shareholders, or the sole shareholder, and one or more managing directors. As a collective body, the general meeting of the shareholders of an LLC consists of all shareholders of the company.

[105] The general meeting/sole shareholder approves all strategic decisions, such as, among others: (i) appointment of managing directors; (ii) change of the article of association; (iii) participation in other companies; (iv) reorganisation or termination of the company. The BCA exhaustively lists the matters, which are in the exclusive competence of the general meeting/sole shareholder. They cannot be delegated to the managing directors. In addition, the articles of association of the company may contain other matters under its exclusive competence.

[106] Depending on the specific matter, the resolutions of the general meeting are adopted with a simple or special majority, or unanimously. Written resolutions in lieu of a meeting are allowed when all shareholders have stated their consent.

[107] An LLC should have one or more managing directors who manage the company and represent it before third parties. Only an individual may be appointed as a managing director of an LLC. There are no restrictions to a foreign person being appointed as a managing director of an LLC.

[108] The managing director organises and manages the day-to-day business of the company in accordance with the law and the resolutions of the general meeting or the sole shareholder.

[109] The managing director is appointed by the general meeting or by the sole shareholder and his/her name should be registered at the CR.

[110] A managing director cannot be an individual who has been:

(i) declared insolvent;
(ii) the managing director or a member of the managing or supervisory body of a company dissolved on grounds of insolvency during the last two years prior to the date of the decision proclaiming insolvency where some creditors have remained unsatisfied;
(iii) the managing director or a member of the managing or supervisory board of a company for which an effective penal ruling has established non-compliance of obligations related to creation and storage of amounts of reserves as specified under the Bulgarian Oil and Oil Products Reserves Act.

Representation of the LLC

[111] An LLC is represented before third parties by the managing director/s. Where several managing directors have been appointed, each of them may act independently, unless the articles of association provide otherwise.

[112] As there is no collective management body (board) in an LLC, the managing director has 'ultimate' power to manage and bind the company, even if he/she exercises powers outside of his/her management contract or internal authorisation. The joint representation (in the case of two or more managing directors or in the event a procurator is appointed) is the only restriction of the director's representation authority binding to third parties.

[113] The articles of association or the management contract may contain other restrictions or limitations of the managing director's representative powers (e.g., restriction on the execution of transactions over a specified amount). However, these restrictions will be effective only in the internal relationships between the managing director and the company. Acting in breach of such restrictions coul trigger the personal liability of the managing director for damages.

[114] The managing directors can authorise third parties by way of a power attorney. The managing directors can specifically authorise proxies with only pa of their representative powers. The issuance of a power of attorney is not subject t registration at the CR or any other institution.

[115] Bulgarian law also recognises the institute of the procurator (in Bulgaria ***прокурист***). According to the BCA, a procurator is an individual authorised to rep resent the company in return for remuneration. The scope of the procurator's rep resentative powers is defined in the BCA. He/she can generally undertake a actions relating to the company's ordinary course of business. Special authorisatio is required for disposal of real estate or for granting of securities over real esta assets. The authorisation should be executed in the form of a notarised power attorney and should be registered at the CR.

Main Rights and Obligations of LLC Shareholders

[116] Each share entitles the shareholder to a voting right, right to dividend right to a liquidation quota upon the company's termination, right to participate i the management of the company, etc. In an LLC the right to vote, the right to div dend and to liquidation quota are proportionate to the share of the capital owne by the shareholder.

[117] The main obligation of a shareholder in an LLC is for a capital contributio in consideration for the shares in the registered capital. In addition, the share holder has an obligation to participate in the management of the company, cooperate for the performance of the company's business and to comply with th resolutions of the general meeting.

General Characteristics of a JSC

Basic Characteristics

[118] A JSC can be formed by one or more Bulgarian or foreign individuals and/ legal entities. The number of founders is not restricted. As with LLCs, JSCs a liable for their obligations with all of the assets and properties belonging to ther The shareholders are not personally liable for the debts of the company.

[119] JSCs can be engaged in all types of commercial activity not prohibited Bulgarian law. JSCs are considered for larger projects where new investors and/ financial institutions may intervene or where the company is likely to engage operations that require accumulation of a greater amount of funds.

Founding and Registration

[120] A JSC is established by the following actions: (i) founding of the JSC at an incorporation meeting where the articles of association are adopted by the shareholders; (ii) payment of the contributions of the shareholders at least in the amount of the legislative minimum; and (iii) registration of the JSC at the CR.

[121] The BCA stipulates the minimum contents of the articles of association, for example, name, seat and registered office, bodies of the company. The articles of association are executed in simple written form.

[122] The shareholders receive interim share certificates for the contributions they have made. Thus, the shareholders receive their shares upon presentation of these interim certificates. In most cases the shareholders exercise their rights only by virtue of the issued interim certificates.

[123] The shareholders in JSCs are not subject to registration with the Commercial Register except for the shareholder in a solely owned JSC. However, the JSC has to keep a shareholders' register where the names and addresses, personal identification number/personal number of non-resident persons or unified identification code of the owners of registered shares are kept recorded. The register also contains information on the type, nominal value and issue price of the shares, their quantity and serial numbers. The Central Depository keeps the shareholders' register of JSCs with dematerialised shares.

Registered Capital of a JSC

[124] The registered capital of a JSC is divided into shares. The BCA stipulates that the minimum amount of the registered capital is equal to BGN50 000 (approximately EUR25 500). A separate legislative act may lay down a higher minimum value of capital for certain JSCs, for example, banks, investment brokers, pension insurance companies. The capital of a JSC should be fully subscribed and at least 25% of the nominal value or issue price of each share must be paid-in before the registration of a JSC at the CR.

[125] The issue price of the shares may differ from the face value, but it cannot be lower than the face value. The difference between the higher issue price and the face value of the shares forms a JSC's share premium reserves.

[126] The shares are undivided and when a share belongs to several persons they must exercise their rights under it jointly, through a proxy.

[127] JSCs can issue registered shares and dematerialised shares. Dematerialised shares are registered shares. Bulgarian law recognises also different types of preferred shares.

[128] Depending on the type of shares, there is a different manner for their transfer. Registered shares are transferred by endorsement. The endorsement must be in writing on the back of the respective share or on a paper attached to the share. In order to be binding to the JSC, the transfer of registered shares must be registered in the company's shareholders book. Dematerialised shares are transferred by virtue of an assignment agreement. The issuance and the transfer of dematerialised shares are effective upon registration in the company's shareholders book, which is kept by the Central Depository.

[129] The transferability of the shares to third parties is not restricted by the BCA. The transfer is free unless otherwise agreed in the articles of association of the JSC.

[130] According to the BCA, two types of capital contributions are allowed:

(i) pecuniary (cash) contributions; and
(ii) in-kind contributions – Like in an LLC, an in-kind contribution made to the JSC is subject to valuation by three independent experts appointed by the CR. The price of the shares that can be subscribed to in the JSC should not exceed the expert valuation of the in-kind contribution. Thus, it can be equal or lower than the valuation amount stipulated by the experts.

Corporate Bodies

[131] JSCs have a complex governance structure comprising a general meeting of shareholders, which consists of all shareholders with a right to vote, and a one-tier or two-tier board system. If a JSC is solely owned by one shareholder, this sole shareholder adopts the resolutions with the competence of the general meeting.

[132] The general meeting decides on all important and significant matters regarding the company, for example, increase and decrease of the registered capital, appointment of the board of directors (one-tier management system) and supervisory board (two-tier management system). The sole shareholder takes these most important decisions if the JSC is solely owned. The general meeting should be held at least once per year for the approval of the annual financial statements.

One-Tier Management System

[133] The management of a JSC with a one-tier management system comprises a board of directors. The number of its members as a collective management body cannot be less than three and not more than nine directors. A director may be an individual or a legal entity. The directors are appointed by the general meeting of the JSC or by the sole shareholder.

[134] The function of the board of directors is to manage and represent the company. The members of the board of directors represent the company jointly, unless the articles of association provide otherwise.

[135] The board of directors can authorise one or more persons as executive directors of the JSC to represent the company before third parties. This is the most common practice in Bulgaria.

[136] The BCA does not impose any restrictions on appointing foreign or non-resident persons as members of the board or executive director/s of a JSC. Where the articles of association allow it, a legal entity may also be appointed as a member of the board, including as an executive director. Where a legal entity is appointed as a member of the board it should appoint an individual who will execute the director's obligations.

Two-Tier Management System

[137] In the two-tier management system, the management bodies of the JSC are a management board and a supervisory board.

[138] The management board consists of at least three members, but not more than nine, which are appointed by the supervisory board. A member of the management board may be an individual or a legal entity. The relationships between the members and the company are set out in written agreements. These agreements are concluded on behalf of the company by the chairman of the supervisory board.

[139] The role of the management board is to manage and represent the company. The managing board, subject to approval of the supervisory board, may authorise one or more persons to serve as legal representatives of the company.

[140] The supervisory board consists of three, but not more than seven members (individuals or legal entities), appointed by the general meeting or sole shareholder of the JSC. The function of the supervisory board is to represent the interests of company's shareholder/s and supervise the activity of the management board.

[141] The law does not provide any restrictions on the appointment of foreign or non-resident persons as members of both management board and the supervisory board. If the articles of association allow it, a legal entity may be appointed as a member of these boards (represented by an individual). However, the same person may not be simultaneously a member of both the management board and the supervisory board.

[142] According to the BCA, a person cannot be elected and registered with the CR as a member of the board of a JSC if he/she/it:

(i) has been a member of a managing or controlling body of a company dissolved on grounds of bankruptcy in the last two years preceding the date of the decision for declaring bankruptcy and there remain unsatisfied creditors;
(ii) had been a managing director, member of management or supervisory body of a company with regard to which non-performance of obligations to constitute and hold stocks under the Crude Oil and Petroleum Products Stocks Act at levels, prescribed for it, had been ascertained by an effective penal decree;
(iii) does not meet other requirements provided for in the articles of association of the JSC.

Representation of a JSC

[143] Typically, the board of directors/management board assigns the management and representation of the company to one or more of its members – executive members (an individual or a legal entity). The executive members have unlimited power to represent the company. In the case of two or more executive members, they can represent the company individually or jointly. Apart from joint represer tation, there are no restrictions on the directors' representative powers effective i relation to third parties.

[144] Internally, the executive members are bound by the decisions of the board (directors/management board. If they act without authorisation, where require (under the law or the articles of association), the transactions would remain vali(and the board members would assume personal liability for any damage caused t the JSC.

[145] In a JSC, business decisions, such as acquisition or disposal of assets, are ger erally within the competence of the management board/board of directors and d not need shareholder approval. As an exception, certain material transactior (such as disposal of the entire business enterprise, assumption of material liabiliti or establishing encumbrances over material assets of the company) require shar holder approval, unless this authority is delegated to the board of directors, whic can take the decision by unanimous vote of its members.

[146] As with an LLC, a JSC can be represented before third parties by a proxy (by a procurator. For more details please *see* paragraphs [112]–[115].

Main Rights and Obligations of the JSC Shareholders

[147] The main obligation of the shareholders in a JSC is to make a capital contr bution in consideration for the subscribed shares of the capital.

[148] Each share entitles the shareholder to a voting right, right to dividend right to a liquidation quota upon the company's termination and right to partic pate in the management of the company. In addition, the shareholders in a JS can be entitled to receive interest on the contribution, a right to subscribe for add tional shares upon an increase in the registered capital, etc.

Public Companies

[149] Under the Bulgarian Public Offering of Securities Act (*POSA*) only a JSC ca be registered as a public company, if it meets any of the following requirements:

(i) has issued shares by an initial public offering (an offer for subscription shares addressed to more than 150 persons); or
(ii) has issued shares registered with the register maintained by the Financi Supervision Commission (*FSC*) for the purpose of their trading on a regu lated market; or
(iii) has more than 10 000 shareholders on the last day of two successive caler dar years; or
(iv) is the surviving company following a merger where at least one of the pa ticipating companies was a public company.

[150] Public companies are registered as such both with the CR and in the regist of the FSC. Every public company should create and maintain its own website.

[151] The POSA establishes a special regime for public companies thus differentiating them from private JSCs. The differences include, among others, the following:

(i) public companies are entitled to distribute a six-month and an annual dividend;

(ii) in order for a shareholder to be entitled to a dividend, it has to be registered in the Central Depository as a shareholder on the fourteenth day from the day of the general meeting at which the six-month or the annual financial statement was adopted and a resolution on profit distribution was passed;

(iii) a public company can only issue dematerialised shares;

(iv) a public company cannot issue preference shares that entitle the shareholder to more than one vote at the general meeting or to an additional liquidation quota;

(v) in the case of a capital increase in a public company, each shareholder has a statutory pre-emptive right. Contrary to the private JSC, this right of the shareholders in public companies cannot be revoked;

(vi) a public company's capital cannot be increased by way of an in-kind contribution or conditionally upon the purchase of the shares by certain persons at a certain price or against debentures issued by the company. The POSA introduces some exception to this rule;

(vii) certain limitations are imposed on directors and representatives of a public company as to the scope of deals they are entitled to conduct without having prior approval of the general meeting. The restrictions stem from the value of every specific deal and its value compared to the balance sheet of the company;

(viii) similar limitations also apply to directors and representatives of a non-public company if it is a subsidiary of a public company. In such cases, the prior approval of the managing body of the public company would be required;

(ix) members of the board of directors and of the supervisory board of a public company have to comply with certain requirements. For example, they cannot be elected if they have been convicted of crimes in relation to ownership, the economy, tax or the social system. A third of the members of the board of directors or of the supervisory board have to qualify as independent from the public company, namely they cannot be an employee of the company, a person in lasting trade relations with the company, a shareholder with at least 25% of the company's shares (or a member of the management or the supervisory board, a procurator or an employee of such shareholder);

(x) every public company appoints an investor relations director. The investor relations director cannot be a member of the board of directors or the supervisory board. He/she is responsible for the effective communication between the board of directors, on the one hand, and the shareholders and potential investors, on the other;

(xi) a company ceases to be a public company as of the date of the Deputy Chairperson of the FSC's decision to deregister this company from the register of public companies. The POSA provides for several cases when deregistration can be triggered, including an explicit unanimous decision of the company's general meeting.

[152] Public companies are required to issue a prospectus for the public offering of their shares. The information contained in the prospectus must be provided in a form easily analysable and comprehensible for investors. Each prospectus should contain information regarding the public company and the shares it emits as well as a resume of the company. The prospectus is subject to mandatory approval by the FSC, which usually takes between four and six weeks.

[153] The transformation of a private JSC into a public company follows strictly a legal procedure, which includes, among others: (i) adoption of a resolution for capital increase by issuance of shares for public offering; (ii) approval of a prospectus; (iii) registration with the register of public companies kept by the FSC; (iv) publication of the prospectus; (v) public offering.

Laws Affecting M&A

Legislative Framework

[154] No particular legislation exists that would specifically regulate M&A matters in all possible aspects. Private and public M&A transactions are mainly regulated by the following acts:

(i) Commercial Act, promulgated in State Gazette No. 48/18 June 1991, effective from 1 July 1991 as amended.
(ii) *POSA*, promulgated in State Gazette No. 114/30 December 1999, effective from 31 January 2000, as amended.
(iii) Council Regulation (EC) No. 2167/2001 of 8 October 2001 on the Statute for a European Company (SE).

[155] In addition, M&A transactions of companies involved in regulated business such as banks and financial institutions, insurance companies, investment companies are regulated by special legislation. Below are some of the main acts that are applicable:

(i) Credit Institutions Act, promulgated in State Gazette No. 59/21 July 2006 effective 1 January 2007, as amended.
(ii) Social Insurance Code, promulgated in State Gazette No. 110/17 December 1999, effective from 1 January 2000, as amended.
(iii) Insurance Code, promulgated in the State Gazette, No. 103/23 December 2005, effective from 1 January 2006, as amended.
(iv) Special Purpose Investment Companies Act, promulgated in State Gazette No. 46/20 May 2003, effective from 1 January 2004, as amended.

(v) Collective Investment Schemes and Other Undertakings for Collective Investments Act, promulgated in State Gazette, No. 77/4 October 2011, as amended.

[156] The above list is not exhaustive as there are other businesses regulated by special legislation. These acts provide for special procedures or requirements for approval, permission and notifications regarding the execution of M&A transactions.

[157] In relation to the different aspects of M&A transactions the following acts may also apply:

(i) Labour Code, promulgated in State Gazette No. 26/1 April 1986, as amended.
(ii) Commercial Register and Register for Non-Profit Legal Entities Act, promulgated in State Gazette No. 34/25 April 2006, effective from 1 July 2007, as amended.
(iii) Accountancy Act, promulgated in State Gazette No. 98/16 November 2001, effective from 1 January 2002, as amended.
(iv) Protection of Competition Act, promulgated in State Gazette No. 102/28 November 2008, as amended.
(v) Civil Procedure Code, promulgated in State Gazette No. 59/20 July 2007, effective from 1 March 2008, as amended.
(vi) Investment Promotion Act, promulgated in State Gazette No. 97/24 October 1997, effective from 24 October 1997, as amended.
(vii) Tax and Social Insurance Procedure Code, promulgated in State Gazette No. 105/29 December 2005, effective from 1 January 2006, as amended.
(viii) CITA, promulgated in State Gazette No. 105/22 December 2006, effective 1 January 2007, as amended.
(ix) Income Taxes on Natural Persons Act (ITNPA), promulgated in State Gazette No. 95/24 November 2006, effective from 1 January 2007, as amended.
(x) AML Act, promulgated in State Gazette No. 27/27 March 2018, as amended.

Reorganisation of Companies: Acquisition of Shares and Businesses

[158] Company reorganisations under the BCA are as follows: (i) reorganisation by way of takeover, merger, division and spin-off; (ii) reorganisation by way of the change of the legal form of the companies; (iii) reorganisation through transfer of assets to the sole shareholder; and (iv) reorganisation with cross-border element, involving companies from countries – Member States of the EU or from other countries – contracting party under the EEA Agreement.

*Takeover (in Bulgarian: **вливане**)*

[159] In the case of reorganisation by way of takeover, all assets of one or more companies (reorganising companies) pass to one existing company (acquiring company). The acquiring company becomes the legal successor of the reorganisin company, which terminates without a winding-up procedure.

Merger (in Bulgarian: **сливане** *)*

[160] In the case of the reorganisation of companies through merger, all assets c two or more companies (reorganising companies) pass to a newly incorporate company, which becomes their legal successor. All reorganising companies term nate without a winding-up procedure.

Division (in Bulgarian: **разделяне***)*

[161] Upon division, all assets of one company (the reorganising company) pass t two or more companies, which become its legal successors. The reorganising con pany terminates without a winding-up procedure.

[162] The companies to which the assets of the reorganising company are tran: ferred could be: (i) existing companies (acquiring companies); (ii) newly incorp(rated companies; or (iii) both existing and newly incorporated.

Spin-Off (in Bulgarian: **отделяне***)*

[163] In the case of a spin-off reorganisation, part of the assets of one compan (reorganising company) passes to one or more companies, which become its leg: successor/s for the respective spun-off part.

[164] The companies that are the legal successor of the assets can be: (i) existin companies; (ii) newly incorporated companies; or (iii) both existing and new incorporated companies.

[165] In contrast to the other three types of reorganisation, the reorganising con pany survives the spin-off.

Spin-Off of a Solely-Owned Company

[166] Upon this special type of spin-off, part of the assets of one company (reorg: nising company) passes to one or more solely owned limited liability or joint-stoc companies (newly incorporated companies). Thus, the reorganising compar becomes the sole owner of the newly incorporated companies' capital. This type (reorganisation could be effected simultaneously with the spin-off under par: graphs [163]–[165].

Basic Characteristics of Takeover, Merger, Division and Spin-Off

[167] The most significant consequence of any form of reorganisation is the leg succession between the reorganising company and the receiving compani (whether newly established or existing companies). Another factor is the avoidan(of liquidation procedure and acquisition of shares in the receiving companies l the shareholders of the reorganising companies.

[168] Upon a company's reorganisation, all transferable property rights and obl gations, rights and obligations under employment relations, factual relations (suc as goodwill, know-how), etc. will pass to the acquiring company. If the reorganising company is terminated as a result of the reorganisation, all permits, licences and concessions issued in its name transfer to the acquiring company by operation of law unless otherwise provided for in special legislation. The legal succession does not apply to the non-transferable rights – i.e., non-transferable by law or by their nature. In most of the cases relating to companies carrying out regulated activities, the respective regulating authority should approve the reorganisation or at least be notified of the anticipated or completed reorganisation.

[169] Takeover and merger are types of reorganisation that are very similar in their legal and economic respects. Therefore, the legislation of some European countries and the Third Council Directive 78/855/EEC do not consider them separate forms of reorganisation.

[170] Completion of takeover or merger requires fulfilment of a number of steps. The participating companies should organise, among others:

(i) signing of a reorganisation agreement in notarised form (i.e., notarisation of signatures);
(ii) preparation of reports of their management bodies;
(iii) adopting corporate resolutions for reorganisation; and
(iv) preparation of reports of the controllers containing the valuation of the exchange ratio.

[171] Further, the reorganisation involves several filings with the CR and is also completed by a final registration with the CR.

[172] Upon both forms of reorganisation, the acquiring company has to manage the assets transferred from the transforming companies separately for a period of six months following completion. This measure aims at protection of the creditors' interests.

[173] Division and spin-off are forms of reorganisation mainly aimed at de-concentration of the company's business. In both forms, one reorganising company carves out part of its assets or business that is transferred to the acquiring companies. The main difference between the forms is that in the case of division the reorganising company winds-up, while the spun-off company continues to exist.

[174] Completion of the division and spin-off also requires the execution of various corporate documents and several filings with the CR. The steps are similar to those by incorporation applicable to takeovers and mergers; however, in the case of a merger and spin-off of a new company, the reorganisation agreement is replaced by a plan of reorganisation.

[175] The creditors' interests are protected through the joint liability of the participating companies for obligations that have arisen before the reorganisation.

Reorganisation by Way of a Change of Legal Form

[176] A company (reorganising company) may transform by changing its legal form, thus converting into a company of another type (newly established company). For example, an LLC can transform into a JSC. The newly established company becomes the legal successor of the transforming company, which terminates without a liquidation procedure. Simultaneously with the change of the legal form, no new shareholders can be accepted.

[177] The main documents to be executed during such reorganisation procedure include, among others: (i) plan for reorganisation in a notarised form (except for reorganisations of a solely owned company); (ii) report of the controller considering the exchange ratio; and (iii) resolution of the reorganising company approving the reorganisation.

[178] The last step in the reorganisation procedure is the registration of the transformation with the CR.

Reorganisation by Way of Transfer of Assets to the Sole Shareholder

[179] All assets of a solely owned company (reorganising company) may transfer to the sole owner if it is an individual registered as a sole proprietor.

[180] The main difference compared to other types of reorganisation is that the successor is not a company but an individual – sole proprietor. The transforming company terminates without liquidation.

[181] The procedure is simplified: only a resolution approving the reorganisation of the transforming company and registration with the CR are required. The resolution should be adopted by the sole owner in writing with notarisation of the signature.

[182] As a measure for creditor protection, the sole proprietor has to manage the assets acquired as a result of the reorganisation separately for a period of six months following completion.

Reorganisation with Cross-Border Elements

[183] The BCA regulates cross-border reorganisation only in the form of takeover and merger, where at least one of the companies involved in the reorganisation has its seat in another Member State of the EU or in a contracting party to the EEA Agreement.

[184] The reorganisation may not be effected if any of the companies involved in the transformation has its seat outside the EU or the law of the Member State governing any of the involved companies does not permit such transformation.

[185] As with the other forms of reorganisation, the procedure includes the execution of certain documents and filings with the commercial registries if a minimum of two different countries are involved.

[186] The main documents that should be drafted for the cross-border merger include: (i) common plan for reorganisation of the involved companies; (ii) managing bodies' report; (iii) report for verification of the common reorganisation plan by the controller for each of the companies; (iv) resolutions approving the reorganisation by each of the companies.

[187] The management body of the acquiring company, if it has its seat in Bulgaria, should apply for registration of the merger with the CR. The application should be accompanied by certificates attesting the proper completion of the pre-merger acts and formalities with respect to the legal entities registered in the other Member States.

[188] If the acquiring company has its seat in another Member State, the reorganising company/ies, which has/have their seat in Bulgaria will be deregistered from the CR.

Acquisition of Shares in LLCs and JSCs

Acquisition of Shares in LLCs

[189] Generally, the transfer of shares from one shareholder to another existing shareholder is unrestricted. However, the articles of association of an LLC may specify mandatory approvals for share transfer among current shareholders. According to the BCA, a share purchase agreement should be executed in the form of a written document with simultaneous notarisation of the signatures and content. This form is required for the validity of the transaction.

[190] The change in the shareholding should be reflected in the articles of association of the respective LLC and is subject to registration with the CR.

[191] The transfer of shares to a third party (i.e., admitting of a new shareholder) should also be executed in the form of a written agreement with simultaneous notarisation of the signatures and content. Such a transfer is conditional on the lack of outstanding payable salaries, employee compensations and statutory social security contributions to employees, including to employees whose employment relationships have been terminated up to three years prior to the share transfer. However, the purchaser of the shares will become a shareholder only if admitted by virtue of a resolution of the general meeting (with a qualified majority of ¾ or more) adopted upon its written application. Unless otherwise provided for in the company's articles of association, the resolution should be executed with a simultaneous notary certification of the content and signatures of the signatories. The new shareholder should accede to the articles of association of the company. The share transfer should then also be registered with the CR.

Acquisition of Shares in JSCs

[192] Depending on the type of shares, Bulgarian legislation provides for different transfer methods.

[193] Registered shares are transferred by way of endorsement. The endorsemer must be in writing on the back of the respective share or on a paper attached to th share certificate. In order to be binding to the JSC, the transfer must be registere in the registered shareholders book. The articles of association may provide fc other conditions for the transfer of registered shares.

[194] Dematerialised shares are transferred by virtue of an assignment agreemen To effect the transfer, a registration in the company's shareholders book kept by th Central Depository is also needed.

[195] Share transfers to third parties are not restricted by the BCA. Thus, th transfer can be considered unrestricted, unless otherwise agreed in the articles c association of the JSC.

Transfer of Going Concern

[196] Under Bulgarian law, a going concern of a company, regardless of the com pany's type, represents an aggregation of rights, obligations and factual relation The rights can include property rights, security rights, receivables and intellectu rights. Bulgarian law may require notifications, registrations, etc., for the transfe of different rights. The obligations could also have a different legal nature and, i most cases correlates with the transferred rights. The factual relations arising out c the trade activity of the company could be the clients' network, know-how, etc.

[197] The entire going concern of a company, or a separate part of it, could be sul ject to transfer. Both should be transferred by virtue of a written contract wit simultaneous notarisation of the signatures and content. Notarisation is require for the validity of the transfer. A going concern with employees can be transferre only after the transferor has paid any outstanding salaries, employee compens tions, and statutory social security contributions of the employees, including t employees whose employment relationships have been terminated up to thre years prior to the transfer of the going concern. The transfer agreement may stipu late that such payments will be made also by the transferee.

[198] If an entire going concern is subject to the transaction, a resolution of th competent body should be adopted with a ¾ majority of the registered capital. N resolution is required for the transfer of a part of a going concern. However, th company's articles of association may require adoption of resolution also in thes cases.

[199] The transferring company is obliged to notify its creditors and debtors of th executed transfer. Upon transfer, unless agreed otherwise by the creditors, th transferring company will be jointly liable with the acquiring company to th amount of the transferred rights.

[200] The transaction should be registered with the CR. The transfer is simult neously announced in the files of both companies. This announcement has only declarative effect towards third parties. Depending on the assets included in th going concern, the transfer may need registration in other registries (e.g., the Lan Registry).

Transfer of Separate Assets: Asset Deal

[201] An asset deal between two companies is another variation of a business transfer, regardless of the type of the companies involved. By virtue of the transaction, separate assets and/or liabilities change their legal owner.

[202] The specific requirements for the transfer of the different assets should be observed. The deal is not subject to registration with the CR but may require registration in other registers depending on the transferred assets (e.g., in the Land Registry if real estate is being transferred).

[203] The difference between a transfer of a going concern and a transfer of individual assets is sometimes truly narrow. However, these transactions may have different tax treatment. Therefore, a careful assessment regarding the legal nature of an asset deal should be made in each specific case in order to mitigate tax risks.

Relevant Regulatory Authorities

Commercial Registry

[204] Companies, branches of foreign companies and non-profit legal entities (such as associations and foundations) and circumstances related thereto are registered at the CR. The CR is managed by the Bulgarian Registry Agency of the Ministry of Justice.

[205] In most cases, the registration of circumstances at the CR has only a declarative effect towards third parties. However, sometimes the registration is required to actually effect the corporate change (e.g., pledge over shares in an LLC).

[206] The applications for registration and deregistration of circumstances or announcement of acts are considered by the officials in the order of their receipt. The applied registration, deregistration or announcement should be executed immediately upon the expiry of three business days following the filing of the documents in the CR. Thus, the respective registration of circumstances and announcement of acts takes not more than five business days. The registration procedure may take longer if the registry officials require additional information or documents.

[207] In the case of registration of a new company, the legislative term is shorter and the registration procedure takes one business day.

Commission for Protection of Competition

[208] In general, the **Commission for Protection of Competition** (CPC) is empowered to enforce the Bulgarian Protection of Competition Act (*PCA*), the Bulgarian Public Procurement Act and the Bulgarian Concessions Act.

[209] The CPC scope of activity covers all requests for ascertaining infringements of effective competition (including, as a result of anticompetitive agreements, abuse of dominance, unfair trade practices or abuse of a stronger bargaining position), review of mergers for their effects on competition, direct enforcement of the provisions of Article 101 and Article 8210 of the Treaty on the Functioning of the EU, cooperation with the European Commission and the other national competition authorities of the EC Member States in conformity to EC Regulation No. 1/2003 and EC Regulation No. 139/2004, conducting sector analyses and competition advocacy.

[210] In relation to M&A transactions, the CPC is the national authority empowered to control concentrations with a national dimension. Thus, when a transaction constitutes a concentration that falls within the scope of PCA, and not within the competence of the European Commission, it should be reported to the CPC.

[211] The following transactions qualify as concentrations:

- *Merger or takeover of two or more independent companies*, i.e., in the case of a merger of two or more previously independent companies into an autonomous economic entity.
- *Acquisition of direct or indirect control over the whole or part of another company.* Control will be constituted by rights (ownership or the right to use all or part of the assets of the company), contracts or any other means which, either separately or in combination and with regard to the considerations of fact or law involved, confer the possibility of exercising decisive influence over a company, including the composition, voting or decisions of the company's bodies.
- *Creation of a joint venture performing sustainably all the functions of an autonomous economic entity:* Where a joint venture is an undertaking over which joint control will be exercised and which has operational independence to perform on an ongoing basis the functions of an economically autonomous entity.

For more details about the merger clearance procedure, please *see* paragraphs [462]–[497].

Central Depository AD

[212] In general, the Central Depository opens and maintains accounts for dematerialised securities, registers transactions with securities, administrates securities including maintaining shareholders books of companies that have dematerialised shares and bonds, etc. The names of the shareholders are recorded in the register of the Central Depository. The institution issues documents certifying the ownership of the dematerialised shares upon request of the owner.

[213] JSCs that have issued dematerialised shares are obliged to register them with the Central Depository. The issuance and disposal of dematerialised securities including dematerialised shares in a JSC, becomes effective after their registration at the Central Depository.

[214] The Central Depository registers the securities within five business days of the receipt of the documents. If the Central Depository has requested additional information, the term starts to run from the provision of these documents and information.

Financial Supervision Commission

[215] The FSC was established on 1 March 2003 under the Bulgarian *FSC* Act. It is an institution that is independent of the government and reports to the National Assembly of the Republic of Bulgaria.

[216] The FSC is a specialised government body for the regulation and control of different segments of the financial system – capital market, insurance market, health insurance market and pension insurance market.

[217] The main responsibilities of the FSC are to regulate and supervise: (i) the activities of the collective investment schemes and enterprises for collective investment; (ii) the public offering of securities, the issue and disposal of dematerialised securities; (iii) the activities of the Central Depository; (iv) the activities of companies with a special investment purpose; (v) the activity of the investment brokers and the activities in the markets of financial instruments.

Bulgarian National Bank

[218] The Bulgarian National Bank is the central bank of the state and reports to the National Assembly. It has been provided with a key role in the Bulgarian economy of maintaining the stability of the Bulgarian currency and of strengthening and development of the banking and credit system in the country.

[219] The most significant mission of the Bulgarian National Bank is to maintain the stability of the banking system and to protect the interests of depositors. The Bulgarian National Bank is the authority issuing licences for execution of banking and non-banking financial activity, controlling and regulating these activities, including reorganisations and the transfer/acquisition of such companies with a special scope of activity.

National Revenue Agency

[220] The National Revenue Agency is the national tax authority that collects taxes and social security contributions. Upon reorganisation of a company and transfer of a going concern, the National Revenue Agency should be notified. The certificate for such notification is a precondition for the registration of the reorganisation/transfer of a going concern with the CR.

Financial Investigations Directorate of the State Agency for National Security

[221] The Financial Investigations Directorate of the State Agency for National Security ('FIDSANS') is a specialised administration responsible for preventing, discovering and counteracting money laundering and the financing of terrorism, including with respect to the movement of capital, corruption, bribery in interna tional transactions and confiscation.

[222] Entities that fall within the scope of the AML Act, such as financial institu tions and payment services providers, must immediately report to FIDSANS an suspicious transactions or other activity they have identified in the course of thei business operations.

Controls/Restrictions on Foreign Investment

Restrictions on Foreign Investments

[223] Bulgarian legislation corresponds to EU principles and guarantees the fre movement of goods, capital, services and people within the EU single marke Therefore, the rules that apply to both national and foreign investors do not diffe

[224] There are no specific authorisations applicable to foreign investments i Bulgaria. Foreign-owned companies must obtain the same authorisations as thos required for domestic companies in certain business sectors. The following is non-exhaustive list of examples:

(i) A credit institution in Bulgaria (such as a bank) may only carry out activiti that are explicitly stipulated in its licence. Authorisation is required i order for these activities to be validly executed: receiving deposits from th public; providing credits or other financing for its own account and at i own risk; providing payment services; acting as a depository or truste institution; trading on its own account or on the account of customers i foreign exchange and precious metals, excluding derivative financi instruments based on foreign exchange and precious metals; etc.

(ii) Manufacturing of and trading in explosives, weapons, ammunition an pyrotechnical products can be conducted by legal entities which are regi tered in Bulgaria or in another Member State. In any case, these activiti require a permit to be granted by the Director of the National Police Dire torate General to the Ministry of Interior.

(iii) For insurance and reinsurance activities conducted in Bulgaria, a licen (issued by the competent authority in Bulgaria or another Member State) required. It comprehensively specifies the type of insurances and oper tions an undertaking could validly conduct. A licence is required regardle of whether the insurer has its seat of business in Bulgaria or in a third sta (and therefore operates in Bulgaria through a duly registered branch However, insurers and reinsurers licensed in another Member State ma operate under the principles of freedom of establishment (through a du registered branch) and freedom to provide services (without the establis ment of a branch), subject to a bespoke notification regime.

(iv) Radio and television broadcasters are subject to licensing and registratio in Bulgaria, regardless of whether they are registered under Bulgarian la or the law of any other Member State. The legal framework imposes restrictions on the issuance of a licence, which are general and do not differ based on the place of registration of the applicant.

(v) Under Bulgarian law, there are activities in the energy sector which are subject to authorisation (production of electricity and/or heat; transmission of electricity, heat and natural gas; distribution of electricity or natural gas; etc.). Authorisation is required for undertakings, which are registered under Bulgarian law or have their seat of business in another Member State. The requirements and the procedure for the obtaining of a licence do not differ.

Formal Approvals

[225] The incorporation of a new company and the acquisition of shares in an existing company (except for in JSCs which are not solely owned) or the reorganisation of an existing company are subject to registration with the CR. The respective corporate change is usually executed immediately upon the expiry of three business days following the filing of the documents with the CR.

[226] The state fees for registration of a new company or corporate change (i.e., acquisition of shares, reorganisation) are different. They depend on the type of company (i.e., LLC or JSC), the type of the requested registration and whether the application for the registration is submitted on paper or electronically. The fees vary between BGN15 and BGN360 (i.e., from approximately EUR8–EUR180).

[227] For a merger filing before the CPC the fees amount to BGN2 000 (approximately EUR1 000) for review of the documentation and, in addition, 0.1% of the total turnover for the previous year of the participants in the concentration, but not more than BGN60 000 (approximately EUR30 000).

[228] The cost for any formal approvals regarding the specific activity of an LLC and JSC varies depending on the type of the activity and the respective procedure (i.e., issuing of licences, permits, registrations and the amendments to them).

Restrictions on Foreign Directors or Managers

[229] Bulgarian legislation does not provide for restrictions regarding the nationality of the managing director/s, executive directors or other members of the managing bodies. No requirements for election of a local director or other members of a company's corporate bodies exist. In addition, no requirements exist for any governmental officials on a supervisory basis.

Trade Permits/Minimum Capital Requirements

[230] Bulgarian legislation provides for minimum capital requirements for an LLC – BGN2 (approximately EUR1) and for a JSC – BGN50 000 (approximately EUR25 000). The minimum amount of the capital does not differ for locally or foreign-owned companies established in Bulgaria. Higher minimum capital requirements are set out in relation to the incorporation of certain regulated entities, such as banks (BGN10 m (approximately EUR5 m), insurance companies (from BGN5 m (approximately EUR2.5 m) to BGN7.4 m (approximately EUR3.7 m)[31], depending on the scope of its licence), etc.

[231] Once incorporated, each LLC and JSC may execute trade activity that is within the scope of business specified in its articles of association/incorporation deed. However, the company may generally perform any trade activity, even if not explicitly mentioned in its scope of activity, which is not prohibited by law and follows the required authorisation (if applicable).

[232] Bulgarian legislation does not envisage permits or other authorisations for foreign-owned companies in order to execute their trade activity in Bulgaria. The same rules apply as for locally owned companies; authorisation is only required where an LLC or JSC pursues a regulated business activity.

Restrictions on Acquisition of Real Estate

[233] In Bulgaria, foreign citizens and foreign companies can acquire buildings, premises within a building and limited property rights (e.g., a construction right and a right of use). Citizens or companies of countries that are members of the EU and EEA may acquire land, including forests, forestlands and agricultural lands in Bulgaria under the same terms applicable to Bulgarian citizens and companies.

[234] Citizens (non-resident citizens) and entities of countries that are not members of the EU and the EEA may acquire ownership title over land, including forests and forestlands, under the terms of an international agreement ratified, promulgated and effective under the terms provided for in the Constitution of the Republic of Bulgaria.

[235] The restrictions on the acquisition of land by foreigners do not apply to Bulgarian legal entities involving foreign participation. Therefore, foreign legal entities and individuals can effectively acquire ownership rights over land through the acquisition of shares or an interest in Bulgarian companies. It is possible for such a company to be 100% owned by a foreign investor.

[236] EU residents and entities, and foreign residents and entities (in case an international agreement between their country of incorporation and Bulgaria has been ratified, promulgated and effective under the terms provided for in the Constitution of the Republic of Bulgaria) may acquire agricultural land in case they or their shareholders have been present in Bulgaria for at least five years before the contemplated acquisition. This rule does not apply to inheritance by law of agricultural lands.

[31] Under limited occasions, i.e. when the licence includes the provision of both life insurances and certain general insurances, the minimum capital requirements in relation to the incorporation of such an insurance company may be up to BGN12.4 m (approximately EUR6.2 m).

[237] Foreigners (non-resident or resident citizens) may acquire ownership title over land, including forests, forestlands and agricultural land in case of inheritance by law. In case of inheritance by law of forests, forestlands or agricultural lands by citizens and entities of countries, which are not members of the EU and the EEA, if not otherwise provided for in an international agreement, have to transfer the ownership to persons who have the right to acquire such estates, within three years of the death of the grantor.

Incentives for Foreign Investment

Grants and Investment Incentives Available to Foreign Investors

[238] A decade ago there was a special regime for the promotion of foreign investments established by the Foreign Investments Act. Following a number of amendments in the regime, currently incentives for investors in Bulgaria are the same for both domestic and foreign companies.

[239] The Investment Promotion Act differentiates investments depending on their size, newly created jobs, the economic sector and region of implementation in certain categories, as follows:

(i) priority class investment;
(ii) class of investment A;
(iii) class of investment B; and
(iv) class of investment C.

A higher class of investment allows the respective investor to benefit from a larger scope of incentive measures, where the fullest scope would be open to a priority class investment.

[240] The Investment Promotion Act provides for supporting measures, which are in line with the EU legal framework on admissibility of state aid. It establishes a system of different categories of investors based on the amount of their investments. It further provides for a number of measures, which aim at stimulating an increasing level of investments in Bulgaria. These measures include, among others:

(i) individual administrative services provided to the investor in shorter terms;
(ii) simplified procedures and lower prices for the sale of publicly owned real estate properties;
(iii) financial assistance by the state for the construction of supporting infrastructure;
(iv) financial assistance by the state for the training of personnel;
(v) financial assistance by the state for reimbursement for social insurance payments made by the investor for personnel;
(vi) tax exemptions under the CITA;

(vii) institutional support (for priority class investments only, where a commi tee of government representatives would be created with respect to the pa ticular investment).

The amount of the investment measures described in items (iv), (v) and (v above is further dependant on the location of the project and in particular on th thresholds of the unemployment rate present at the respective municipality. A investor benefits from the largest amount of these investment measures if it impl ments its project in municipalities with the highest rate of unemployment. A ma of the unemployment rate per municipality is periodically updated and public available.

The measures would not be applicable to foreign investors if in its home countr the investor:

(i) has been convicted for a crime by an enforceable sentence, unless rehabil tated;
(ii) has been adjudicated insolvent or is subject to pending insolvency procee ings or has made an out-of-court arrangement with the creditors there within the meaning of the Bulgarian Commerce Act;
(iii) is subject to pending liquidation proceedings;
(iv) has pecuniary obligations to the state or to a municipality which are esta lished by an enforceable act of a competent authority, save as where rescheduling or deferral of the said obligations has been allowed;
(v) has outstanding payments for labour remunerations to employees an these payments are established by an enforceable penalty decree.

These restrictions apply equally to domestic investors.

[241] The certificate for the class of the investment is granted under an admini trative procedure by the Minister of Economy, Energy and Tourism through bespoke agency called InvestBulgaria Agency. After obtaining the certificate, th investor should enter into an agreement with the Bulgarian state.

[242] By virtue of an explicit provision in the Investments Promotion Act, if the is a more favourable regime provided for in an international treaty or a bilater agreement, it should be applicable and not the Investments Promotion Act itself

Special Economic Zones

[243] By virtue of Decree No. 2242 on Free Zones (promulgated in State Gazet No. 55 of 17 July 1987, last amendments promulgated in State Gazette No. 113 28 December 2004) free economic zones can be established on Bulgarian territor The aim of such free zones is to encourage business initiatives for the manufactu ing of goods, the rendering of services, and commercial and other activities nece sary for the diversification and increase of exports.

[244] Where a free zone is established:

(i) all economic activities are exempted from customs duties;

(ii) all payments related to activities conducted on its territory are made in freely convertible currency;
(iii) any property of foreign legal entities and natural persons may not be subject to appropriation or confiscation by an administrative procedure.

[245] Currently there are six active free zones in Bulgaria:

(i) Bourgas Free Zone – this is the only free zone along the Bulgarian Black Sea coast.
(ii) Vidin Free Zone – located on the Danube coast close to the Vidin-Kalafat Ferry complex and next to the Vidin Cargo port.
(iii) Dragoman Free Zone – located close to the Bulgarian-Serbian border.
(iv) Plovdiv Free Zone – strategically located not only in the heart of Bulgaria but in the heart of the Balkan Peninsula close to a number of international roads.
(v) Ruse Free Zone – located on the Danube coast right next to Danube I Bridge and to the largest river port in Bulgaria (Ruse East Port).
(vi) Svilengrad Free Zone – located two kilometres from the Bulgarian-Greek border and 50 meters from the railway connections Bulgaria–Turkey and Bulgaria–Greece. The plot provides direct access to Pan-European Transport Corridor No. 10.

Guarantees Against Expropriation or Nationalisation: Repatriation of Profits

Guarantees Against Expropriation or Nationalisation

[246] The Bulgarian Constitution guarantees private property, irrespective of the nature of the ownership, and any expropriation measures are restricted. The Constitution proclaims the inviolability of private property.

[247] Forcible expropriation of property in the name of the Bulgarian state or municipal needs could be effected only by virtue of a law, provided that these needs cannot be otherwise met, and after fair compensation has been ensured in advance.

[248] These general rules are further detailed in the Bulgarian legislation. There are explicit procedures that have to be strictly followed when expropriation measures are undertaken.

[249] Bulgaria is also a party to the Convention on the Settlement of Investment Disputes between States and Nationals of Other States, establishing the International Centre for Settlement of Investment Disputes (*ICSID) Convention* and has ratified a number of bilateral investment treaties, which usually provide supplementary guarantees against expropriation, nationalisation and measures with equivalent effect.

Payment of Dividends and Repatriation of Profit

[250] Payment of dividends and repatriation of profits or proceeds of liquidation or sale follow the same procedures for both local and foreign investors.

[251] The following sources of income, among others, are considered profit anc income from a source inside Bulgaria and are therefore subject to a mandatory withholding tax:

(i) any profits of non-resident legal persons which derive from the economic activity carried out through a permanent establishment in Bulgaria or fron the disposition of property of any such permanent establishment (the amount of the mandatory withholding tax is 10%);

(ii) any income from dividends and shares in a liquidation surplus, deriving from interests from participation in resident legal entities in Bulgaria (the amount of the mandatory withholding tax is 5%);

(iii) any copyright and licence royalties accumulated in favour of non-residen legal entities (the amount of the mandatory withholding tax is 10%).

[252] Depending on the state of which the foreign investor is a citizen of (when the investor is an individual) or where the legal entity has its seat of business, double tax treaties may be applicable.

[253] Every trans-border bank transfer or payment to a third party in an amoun of BGN30 000 (approximately EUR16 000) or the equivalent in any other currency or higher has to be accompanied by certain documents required by law. Such docu ments aim at certifying the grounds for the transfer as well as the amount being transferred. A declaration in standard form is also required to accompany the set o documents.

[254] Individuals are allowed to carry unlimited quantities of cash across the Bul garian state border. If the amount exceeds EUR10 000 or its equivalent in another currency and the money is transferred to or from a non-EU Member State, the exact amount is subject to a declaration before the customs authorities. Further more, in the event that an individual intends to carry an amount exceeding BGN3(000 (approximately EUR16 000) across the Bulgarian state to a non-EU Membe State and outstanding public liabilities of such an individual are established, the customs authorities would not allow him/her to export the amount. Declaring o the amount is up to the discretion of the competent authorities if the transfer is tc or from a Member State and the amount exceeds EUR10 000. Any failure to com ply with these obligations could constitute either a criminal offence or an adminis trative violation, depending on the factual and legal background.

[255] Cash payments in Bulgaria cannot exceed in one transaction BGN10 00((approximately EUR5 000) or its equivalent in another currency. This restrictior also applies when an instalment under a contract is below the threshold if the tota due amount under the contract exceeds BGN10 000.

Financing Options for Acquisitions by Foreign Investors in Bulgaria

[256] Financing options could be:

(i) *Loans* – These are provided mainly by credit institutions against some sor of security or guarantee (such as pledges of movable property; pledges o going concerns; pledges of shares; pledges of receivables; mortgages o real estate; mortgages of ships; promissory notes; guarantors (including both parent companies and/or subsidiaries acting in this capacity); co-debtors). It is not unusual for an acquisition in Bulgaria to be financed by a foreign bank. It is permissible for a foreign lender to take security over local immovable property. The ban on foreigners or foreign entities owning agricultural land does not interfere with such a conclusion as Bulgarian law does not provide for a possibility of a lender to directly acquire an ownership title over security provided by a borrower if the latter is non-performing. The security, i.e., the agricultural land, would be offered for public sale. The lender would be compensated monetarily for the non-performance of its contracting party.

(ii) *Bonds* – This option is only open to joint-stock companies. The company issues bonds and so receives financial support. The issued bonds can be backed only by the general creditworthiness and reputation of the issuing company (in the case of debentures) or could be issued against some form of security or guarantee. Subject to certain requirements, bonds can convert into shares in the company's capital.

(iii) *Capital increase* – The company can increase its capital by attracting new investors who subscribe to its shares. The capital increase can provide some cash for the finances of the company.

Specific Issues of Company/Securities Law

Shareholder Approval of M&A Transactions

[257] Entering into M&A transactions is subject to the specific restrictions set out in the BCA and the articles of association of each company.

[258] In a JSC certain material transactions (such as disposal of the entire business enterprise, assumption of material liabilities or establishing encumbrances over material assets of the company) require shareholder approval, unless this authority is delegated to the board of directors, which can take the decision by unanimous vote of its members. Respectively, where the JSC has a two-tier management system, the decision can be taken after the management board has obtained the consent of the supervisory board. There are no such requirements for LLCs, however usually similar limitations are included in the companies' articles of association.

[259] Purchase of shares in an LLC (if less than 100% of the registered capital is acquired) requires the approval of the general meeting.

[260] The approval of a merger or a spin-off by the shareholders requires special majorities. For an LLC the reorganisation is approved by the shareholders representing three-quarter of the company's registered capital unless a higher majority is provided under the company's articles of association. The merger or spin-off of a JSC requires a majority of ¾ of the shares presented at the general meeting unless a higher majority is provided for in its articles of association.

Form of Consideration

[261] According to the BCA, two types of contributions are allowed against th subscribed shares in capital companies (i.e., LLCs and JSCs) – pecuniary (cash cor tributions) and in-kind contributions.

[262] In-kind contributions are allowed upon incorporation of a new company c upon subscription of newly issued shares in an existing company. The contribu tions are the source of the company's property and therefore should be materi and valuable. Thus, the in-kind contributions can consist of tangible assets: prop erty rights (ownership title, limited property rights, receivables, shares, securities intangible assets – trademarks, industrial design, patents, licences, know-how, et

[263] Future work or services are explicitly banned from being subject to in-kin contribution.

[264] The execution of an in-kind contribution is regulated by specific rules aime at protecting the company from decapitalisation.

[265] The in-kind contributions in LLCs and JSCs are subject to valuation by thre experts appointed by the CR's officials. The expert report should contain a fu description of the in-kind contribution, the evaluation method, the valuation of th in-kind contribution and the ratio between the value of the contribution and th number of shares/quotas that will be subscribed by the shareholder/s. During th valuation procedure, the contributor should prove its ownership over the right sub ject to in-kind contribution.

[266] The price of the shares/quotas subscribed against an in-kind contributio should not exceed the experts' valuation of the contribution.

[267] As required by law, the articles of association/incorporation deed should cor tain the name of the contributor (i.e., the shareholder), full description of th in-kind contribution, its valuation and the grounds of its rights (e.g., notary dee contract for the respective receivable).

[268] The shares/quotas, regardless of whether acquired against an in-kind or cash contribution, can be transferred in the same way. No consequent restrictior on disposal of shares acquired through in-kind contribution are provided in Bu garian legislation.

Financial Assistance

[269] Up and cross-stream securities (in rem and guarantee) are a typical feature security packages in a buy-out scenario under Bulgarian law. Although there is n explicit rule with respect to 'capital maintenance', as in other jurisdictions, the BC prohibits the shareholders from claiming back their capital. This could restrain th provision of grantees and security interest by a company to a parent company c third parties. In the case of up and cross-stream guarantees, limitation language often applied in the credit facility documentation in order to preserve the regis tered capital of the company.

[270] The BCA, implementing the provisions of the Second Company Directive, prohibits the granting of loans or the provision of security (in rem or guarantees) by a JSC for the acquisition of its own shares. Such loans and security may be declared void, even if they are not directly provided by the target company (e.g., channelled through a third party). Bulgaria has not implemented the subsequent easements in the European framework regarding financial assistance; therefore, no distinction is made between the regime for public and private JSC. Additionally, no whitewashing procedures are established in order to clear the extension of a loan or granting of security for the purchase of the shares of the JSC. No financial assistance rules exist for other corporate forms such as an LLC or a limited partnership.

[271] As a practical matter, this absolute prohibition can be overcome by the extension of working capital facilities or the refinancing of existing debt at the level of the JSC, which could be considered a tangible 'corporate benefit', representing an adequate consideration. Additionally, a change in corporate form from a JSC to an LLC is sometimes used in order to overcome this problem.

Security Interests

[272] Other than the traditional division between personal and in rem security, the main distinction of security interest with respect to the type of security assets, as in other civil law jurisdictions, are security over movables and security over real estate.

Mortgage

[273] A mortgage (in Bulgarian: ***ипотека***) represents a security interest over a real estate or a ship with the mortgage being effective upon its registration in the Land Registry. The mortgagor keeps possession of the real estate until the beginning of a foreclosure proceeding. Arguably, the security interest over real estate under Bulgarian law could be regarded as conservative and cost-intensive as the foreclosure procedure is quite formalistic and requires a public sale. The statutory term for the duration of a mortgage is ten years, with an option to re-register the mortgage before this term lapses. If the mortgage is not renewed prior to the end of the term or after the term, the mortgagor may lose its ranking (e.g., if other mortgages have been established in the meantime).

Pledge

[274] A pledge (in Bulgarian: *залог*) is a contract in which a pledgor transfers to a pledgee the possession of a movable asset (e.g., movable assets, receivables, shares) as a security interest for the repayment of a debt. No act for perfection is needed other than the simple handing over of the asset, or the instrument incorporating it, to the pledgee. As a matter of practice, the pledge will be in the form of a notarised written contract. Additionally, registered shares are handed over to the pledgee with an endorsement in the pledge. Registration in the company's shareholders book is also required. As for book entry (dematerialised) securities, the pledge should be registered in the Central Depository in order to perfect the security interest.

Non-possessory Pledges

[275] As a possessory pledge is regarded as inflexible, because of the transfer of possession, a Registered Pledges Act was enacted that establishes a modern 'non-possessory' type of security interest. It does not require any act of perfection, such as handing over of the asset, other than a notarised form of the security agreement and a book entry into a special register – the Central Registered Pledges Register. Examples of such type of 'non-possessory' security interest under the Registered Pledges Act are:

(i) pledge over a floating pool of movables or receivables (in Bulgarian: ***залог върху съвкупност***);
(ii) pledge over dematerialised securities (in Bulgarian: ***залог върху безналични ценни книги***);
(iii) going concern pledge (in Bulgarian: ***залог на търговско предприятие***);
(iv) pledge over share quotas in an *LLC* (in Bulgarian: ***залог на дялове***);
(v) pledge over receivables (in Bulgarian: ***залог на вземания***).

[276] Both a mortgage and pledge (possessory and non-possessory) are considered accessory to the underlying claim. They are established only when the primary obligation comes into existence and are discharged upon the discharge of the 'primary' obligation. The principle of accessoriness under Bulgarian law does not allow a transfer of the security interest separately from the secured claim and strictly follows its 'life'. If accessory security is granted for a future claim, it comes into existence only if the claim is established. Moreover, the concept of the unity of a creditor and holder of the security is so entrenched in Bulgarian jurisprudence that the terms 'creditor' and 'mortgagee/pledgee' are used interchangeably in the legislative acts. Essentially, only a bank guarantee can be arranged as non-accessory. This is problematic in cases of syndication, secondary debt trading or where a bridge loan will be refinanced by a bond issue, as the security will have to be granted to the new creditor. Parallel debt structures governed by foreign law, usually English law, are often used in the credit agreement to overcome this problem.

[277] The Registered Pledges Act has introduced security interests, similar to the fixed and floating charges, such as the generic granting of a security interest over all the assets of a company or a pool of receivables. In these types of security interests, the assets, specifically listed in the pledge agreement, are 'fixed' and the security will 'follow' them before the enforcement. The other assets in the floating pool could fluctuate and only the unlisted assets that are owned by the company upon the commencement of the enforcement will 'crystalize'. Moreover, a registered pledge is the preferred choice for a security interest because it provides an out-of-court procedure for the private sale of the pledged assets by the pledgee for the account of the pledger. The proceeds are then disbursed to a special receiver (depository) for distribution to all of the creditors.

[278] Under the Bulgarian ladder of priorities, a security interest provides a first ranking position for the satisfaction of the creditors' claims, which cannot be impaired by any claims by public authorities or employees. This 'super-senior' position of a secured creditor in an insolvency scenario is mitigated by a specific mechanism in the insolvency procedure. The insolvency administrator or any other insolvency creditor, if the administrator fails to act, could challenge the granting of security to a creditor which: (i) was established within the suspicious periods; (ii) is detrimental to the other creditors of the company; and (iii) did not have commercial reasoning.

[279] The suspect period for the creation of a mortgage or a pledge to secure a previously unsecured claim against an insolvent debtor starts from the earlier of (i) one year from to the filing of the petition for opening of the insolvency proceedings; and (ii) the initial date of the illiquidity/over-indebtedness, as determined by the court.

[280] Upon petition of the insolvency administrator or any other insolvency creditor, if the administrator fails to act, a pledge, mortgage or the granting of a personal guarantee to secure a third-party obligation established within one year prior to the date of filing the petition for the opening of the insolvency proceedings, but not earlier than the initial date of insolvency/over-indebtedness, could be invalidated by the court.

[281] Upon petition of the insolvency administrator or any other insolvency creditor, if the administrator fails to act, the creation of a pledge or mortgage or the granting of a personal guarantee as a security to third-party obligations in favour of a creditor related to the insolvent debtor provided within the two-year period prior to the date of the petition for opening of the insolvency proceedings could be invalidated by the court.

Completion Formalities

[282] The particular formalities required to effect the transfer of shares in an LLC and a JSC has been specified in paragraphs [189]–[195] above.

[283] Bulgarian legislation requires that each transaction concerning ownership title over immovable property must be executed by virtue of a notary deed. This includes the transfer of real estate properties and establishment of limited real estate rights (e.g., rights of use and construction right).

[284] Since the notary deed is a special transaction document, it should be executed before a notary public registered in the region where the real estate is located. After its execution, the notary deed should be registered with the Land Registry in order to make the purchaser's title defendable against third parties.

[285] In some cases an exception to the requirement for a notary deed exists. The sale of a going concern containing real estate property and the in-kind contribution of a real estate property is executed in the form of a written document with notarisation of the signatures. In addition, a notary deed is not required for the sale and purchase of municipal or state immovable property where the simple written form is sufficient for the lawful transfer of the ownership title. However, registration of the transaction with the Land Registry is still required.

[286] Bulgarian legislation stipulates special rules for transactions with real estat properties under special procedures such as insolvency, enforcement.

[287] Bulgarian legislation does not provide a special form for the transfer of th ownership over movable assets, with only a few exceptions (e.g., for transfer c motor vehicles).

[288] In practice, the transfer of receivables is executed in the form of a writte agreement, which simplifies the proof of the transaction. The assignment of receiv ables secured by a mortgage, however, requires notary certification of the signa tures in order to make the assignment effective also with respect to the mortgag The receivables are transferred to the new creditor along with its privileges, secu rities and other attributes, including interest arrears unless otherwise agreed. Th former creditor must notify the debtor of the transfer and hand over to the ne creditor any documents it may hold which verify the claim, as well as a confirmatio in writing that the transfer has taken place. A transfer shall be binding upon thir parties and the debtor from the date when the debtor is notified by the forme creditor.

Costs and Fees

[289] The main costs and fees regarding M&A transactions are notary fees fo notarisation of signatures and documents, translation fees and state fees for regis tration with the CR or another registry (if applicable). The notifications, announce ments and registration procedures have been specified in paragraphs [205]–[220 above. No disclosure obligations concerning the acquisition of a substantial hold ing of shares exist unless the target is a public company or is engaged in certai regulated businesses (banks, financial institutions, insurance companies, etc.)

Dividends

[290] Shareholders in LLCs and JSCs are entitled to receive part of the profit o the company annually and to acquire a liquidation quota in the event of liquidatio of the company.

[291] Distribution of dividends is possible only after the closing of the curren financial year, the evidence of a positive financial result and the adoption of a reso lution by the shareholder/s approving of the annual financial statements and th distribution of profit.

[292] Although not explicitly regulated by law, it is sometimes accepted that upo certain conditions the general meeting of the shareholders or the sole shareholde in an LLC may approve interim distributions, which are different from the distri bution of profit. These preliminary payments depend on the estimated profit o the LLC, and they are often based on an interim balance sheet. In any case, thes preliminary payments should not result in the decapitalisation of the company. I contrast to an LLC, preliminary payments (i.e., payments different from the annua distribution of profit) are not permitted in a JSC.

[293] The right to dividends derives from the participation in the company or from the ownership of the shares. Therefore, no restrictions regarding the nationality of the shareholder/s exist when the dividends are paid.

[294] An LLC does not form reserves, unlike a JSC. Furthermore, the formation of reserves is a legislative obligation for JSCs. At least one-tenth of a JSC's profit should be allocated to the reserves fund until the amount of the fund accumulates to at least one-tenth of the capital. Thus, retained profit cannot be distributed until the legislative minimum of reserves is reached. Since an LLC does not maintain reserves, these limitations regarding the distribution of profit are not applicable.

Purchase of Own Shares

Acquisition or Redemption of Own Shares

[295] The BCA provides for the acquisition of own shares only in a JSC upon fulfilment of the legislative requirements. Thus, the acquisition or redemption of own shares in an LLC is restricted.

[296] The cases where a JSC may purchase own shares are explicitly listed in the CA as follows:

(i) Decrease in the JSC's registered capital.
In this case the shares are purchased back by the company in order to be invalidated. Thus, the capital is effectively decreased. The general meeting of shareholders should adopt a prior resolution for the decrease in the registered capital by this means.

(ii) Upon legal succession, except for reorganisation.
The company can become a legal successor of own shares upon inheritance by will or if the company acquires a going concern, containing its own shares.

(iii) Purchase of its own shares without consideration.

(iv) A JSC is involved in securities transactions by occupation and acquires the shares upon order of a third person.
A JSC that executes transactions with securities may acquire its own shares following a third party order, i.e., in the name of the JSC, but for the account of a third party. The investment brokers execute transactions for the account of another person by occupation. As investment brokers, a JSC could acquire its own shares on its behalf and become their bearers. On the grounds of contracts with their clients they are obliged to transfer the acquired own shares to them. During the period when they are bearers of the shares, they should not execute the rights under them.

(v) Upon dismissal of a shareholder.
If a shareholder does not execute its capital contributions due within the specified term (i.e., one month of the written notice to do so), it is considered dismissed. The dismissed shareholder loses its shares in the JSC and capital contributions already made. These shares are acquired by the JSC, but it cannot exercise the rights under the shares. It has to annul and invalidate the shares and to offer for sale new shares substituting the annulled

ones. The contributions made by the dismissed shareholder are allocated to the reserves of the JSC.

(vi) Result of enforcement of a shareholder's obligation to the JSC.
The shareholder could be in default under an obligation towards the JSC. The obligation may arise from a contractual or non-contractual relationship between the shareholder and the company. If the shareholder does not voluntarily execute its obligations, the company is entitled to proceed to enforcement. Therefore, JSC may enforce over its own shares and subsequently acquire shares, if the JSC participates in the enforcement procedure.

(vii) Shares are issued as privileged shares for the purpose of being acquired by the company;
The acquisition of own shares issued as privileged shares is a form of redemption of shares. Its characteristics are specified in detail in paragraph [296] (viii).

(viii) Redemption of own shares.

A JSC may redeem its own shares on the basis of a general meeting resolution, which should specify:

- the maximum number of shares subject to redemption;
- the terms and conditions under which the management body will execute the redemption. The term cannot be longer than five years;
- the minimum and maximum amount of the price for the share redemption.

The resolution should be adopted by a majority of the present capital. If the redemption is not explicitly provided for in the articles of association, then a majority of two-thirds is required. The resolution should be registered at the CR.

General Requirements for the Acquisition of Own Shares

[297] According to Bulgarian law, upon the acquisition of own shares under items (iii), (iv), (vi), (vii) and (viii) above, the shares should be fully paid-in. In all cases, the company should not exercise the rights under the shares until their transfer.

[298] The total nominal value of the acquired own shares, except for those received upon a decrease in the registered capital, should not exceed 10% of the registered capital. The JSC has to transfer the number of own shares exceeding the maximum threshold within a period of three years. If the shares, acquired under item from (ii) to (viii) above are not transferred within the required term, they should be invalidated and the registered capital should be decreased accordingly.

[299] If the company acquires own shares in violation of the rules above, it has to transfer them within one year of the acquisition date. Otherwise, the shares will be invalidated through the procedure of decreasing the company's capital.

[300] Public companies can acquire own shares up to 3% of the registered capital for one calendar year. Special limitations apply also for the acquisition procedure, the disposal of own shares, etc.

Piercing the Corporate Veil

[301] The concept of piercing the corporate veil is not recognised under Bulgarian law. The shareholders in the most often used companies (LLC and JSC) are responsible for making their contributions to the company, not to the creditors of the company. Thus, shareholders cannot be held liable for the debts or other liabilities of the company. The risk for shareholders is that they lose their investment.

[302] The BCA provides for joint liability of the founders of an LLC for damage caused upon its incorporation (i.e., before the registration of the company with the CR) if they have not acted with due care. The liability is not limited to the capital contribution. Practical examples for liability could be: (i) the founders have assumed obligations on behalf of the company causing the company's decapitalisation; (ii) actions damaging the reputation of the company, etc.

Insolvency

General Overview of the Insolvency Proceedings

[303] A Bulgarian company qualifies as insolvent where it is either: (i) illiquid or; (ii) over-indebted, and such circumstances are not temporary.

[304] A company is illiquid when it is unable to meet its due monetary obligations arising out of: (i) commercial transactions; or (ii) a public relationship with the state or the municipalities related to its commercial activity (e.g., taxes); or (iii) a private relationship with the state; or (iv) an employment relationship with at least one-third of the employees, when the obligations have not been met for at least two months. It is assumed that the company is illiquid if it has stopped making its payments.

[305] A company is over-indebted when the company's assets are insufficient to cover the company's monetary obligations. Over-indebtedness is determined based on the company's assets and liabilities pursuant to the latest financial statements of the company as well as pursuant to valuation of the company's assets and liabilities at the time when the request for opening of insolvency is submitted.

[306] The court decides whether a company qualifies as insolvent based on evidence presented by the company (where the request is filed by the company) or by its creditors (where the request is filed by a creditor).

[307] The court decision leads to the suspension of any court enforcement proceedings, initiated against the debtor's assets that are included in the insolvency estate, as determined by the ruling of the court. The creditors, having a valid claim against the company, become creditors of the insolvency estate and the enforcement of their rights takes place through the insolvency procedures.

Distressed M&A

[308] When purchasing company shares in a distressed company, it should be noted that according to Bulgarian law all shareholder loans would be subject to equitable subordination upon insolvency (i.e., there are no statutory thresholds fo shareholder loans).

[309] There is no prohibition under Bulgarian law of the sale of the shares of a insolvent company. This could be done directly by the shareholders, as this woul not change the position of the company. However, often the shares of a distresse company are pledged in favour of some of its creditors. If this is the case, an agree ment with the creditors will be needed. Also, the sale of shares in LLC will only b possible if there are no outstanding payments relating to salaries, employee com pensations or social security contributions. A buyer can acquire shares in a com pany (e.g., operating subsidiary) owned by a company which is in an insolvenc procedure, but this transaction should be concluded with the insolvency trustee c the holding company.

[310] Additionally, in insolvency proceedings shareholders, creditors or the inso vency trustee can present a restructuring plan. The plan can envisage among oth ers the sale of the whole or part of the going concern of the insolvent company o debt-to-equity conversion. The detailed plan should be approved by the insolvenc court. It must include an assessment of the market value of the assets constitutin the going concern and the portion of the liabilities that will be transferred with i together with an executory version of the sale agreement.

Choice of Law/Jurisdiction

[311] As per the Bulgarian Private International Law Code, Bulgarian courts hav exclusive jurisdiction over court cases regarding any actions for the establishmen of inadmissibility or nullity of a company's registration, as well as for non-existenc of registered circumstances when the company is registered in Bulgaria. The Bu garian courts are also exclusively competent in the case of court claims for th validity or termination of a company, revocation of acts of a company's bodies, pro tection of membership, as well as for the reorganisation of a company and for mon etary settlement upon reorganisation when the company is registered in Bulgaria

[312] Where an action is brought to assert a property right and the dispute doe not fall within the exclusive jurisdiction of the Bulgarian courts, any such actio may be submitted to a foreign court by an agreement in writing between the par ties. Where the Bulgarian court has been called while such an agreement is i place, the defendant must raise its objection to exercise such jurisdiction within th time limit for response to the statement of action and before the court has taken stand on the merits of the dispute. Unless otherwise is provided for by the agree ment, it will be presumed to provide the Bulgarian or foreign courts with exclusiv jurisdiction over the dispute for the subject matter covered by the said agreemen

[313] Matters regarding companies registered in Bulgaria are governed by Bulgar ian law. Thus, Bulgarian law regulates: (i) the incorporation, legal nature and lega form of the company; (ii) the name, legal personality and management system o the company; (iii) the composition, competence and functioning of the company' bodies; (iv) representation; (v) the acquisition or loss of membership, as well as th related rights and obligations; (vi) obligations, liability and consequences of

breach of the law and the articles of association; and (vii) the reorganisation and termination of the company.

[314] Generally, in most of the matters concerning establishing companies in Bulgaria or transfer of shares in Bulgarian companies, the applicable law will be Bulgarian law.

[315] Regarding a contractual arrangement (such as an acquisition agreement), the parties are free to choose another governing law. Any such choice must be expressed or clearly demonstrated by the terms of the contract or by the circumstances under which the contractual relationship evolves.

[316] At their discretion, the parties can select a governing law applicable to the whole or a part of the contract. However, where all the elements of a contract at the time of choice are connected with one state only, the choice of foreign law must not prejudice the application of the mandatory rules of this state, which cannot be derogated from by the contract.

[317] The parties to a property dispute (i.e., including trade claims) may agree that such dispute will be settled by an arbitration court unless the dispute has as its subject matter any real estate rights or possession of real estate property, maintenance obligations or rights under an employment relationship. The arbitration agreement should be in writing.

[318] If both parties (individuals or companies) to a contract are resident or have their seat in Bulgaria (including a company with foreign participation) the agreed arbitration court should also be in Bulgaria. The arbitration may have a seat abroad if at least one of the parties has its residence or seat according to its articles of association or place of actual management abroad.

Specific Rules on Public Takeovers

Legislative Framework and Competent Authority

[319] In Bulgaria, public takeovers are regulated by the POSA, which transposes the provisions of Directive 2004/25/EC of the European Parliament and of the Council of 21 April 2004 on takeover bids (the Takeover Directive).

[320] Some subsidiary provisions can also be found in Ordinance No. 13, dated 22 December 2003 relating to tender offers for the buying and exchanging of shares.

[321] The competent authority designated to regulate and control public takeovers is the FSC, which is a specialised governmental body for regulation and control over different segments of the financial system (for more details please *see* paragraphs [215]–[217]).

[322] In certain cases where a concentration approval is required, the CPC can provide such approval. There might be other institutions involved with respect to different elements of an anticipated transaction, such as the Bulgarian Stock

Exchange (which adopts general provisions on public takeovers, registers the transactions, etc.) and the Central Depository (keeps records of public companies equity and shares, provides settlement of corporate securities, etc.)

Specific Requirements

[323] The public takeover rules apply to acquisition of 'control' (for a definition of control, please *see* below) in joint-stock companies listed on the Bulgarian Stock Exchange.

[324] The provisions stipulated in the POSA do not apply to tender offerings regarding:

(i) securities issued by companies whose purpose is collective investment of funds raised through the public offering of shares, operating on the principle of risk-spreading, and on request from holders of such shares to buy-back directly or indirectly their shares at a price based on their net asset value;
(ii) shares issued by the central banks of EU Member States.

[325] One of the main characteristics of the public takeover rules regulated in the POSA is that they apply only in cases of acquisition of control in a public company. Within the meaning of the POSA, control is in place every time a person:

(i) holds, *inter alia,* through a subsidiary or by virtue of an agreement entered into with another person, more than 50% of the number of votes of the general meeting of a company or other legal person; or
(ii) may designate, whether directly or indirectly, more than one-half of the members of the management body or the supervisory body of a legal person; or
(iii) may in any other way exercise a decisive influence over decision making in connection with the business of a legal person.

Principles of Public Takeovers

[326] Under the POSA, the following principles should be observed in the course of every public takeover:

(i) Ensuring equal treatment of the shareholders enjoying equal status in the target company and protection of other shareholders upon acquisition of control of the company.
(ii) Allowing sufficient time and providing sufficient information to the shareholders of the company as may be needed for an informed assessment of the offer and for making a reasoned decision regarding acceptance of the said offer. When providing its reasoned opinion, the management body of the target company must provide its opinion regarding the consequences

arising out of the acceptance of the tender offer in relation to the employees, the conditions of the employment contracts and the place of business activity of the target company.

(iii) The management bodies must act in the best interest of the company as a whole, without preventing the shareholders from being able to take a decision on the substance of the tender offer;

(iv) Not allowing market manipulation in the securities of the company subject to a tender offer, as well as in other companies affected by the tender offer.

(v) Making a tender offer only after the bidder is able to pay the full price for the purchase or the exchange, as the case may be, of the shares to the shareholders who have accepted the offer;

(vi) The target company should not be placed in a situation which inhibits its activity for an unjustifiably long period of time.

Available Takeover Structures

[327] In principle, three types of public takeovers may be differentiated under the POSA:

(i) mandatory bids, which cover situations where there is an obligation for a bid to be performed;

(ii) voluntary bids where there is a possibility for a bid to be performed; and

(iii) squeeze-out or buy-out initiated by minority shareholders following a successful bid in a public company.

[328] The advantages or disadvantages of these procedures (each to be discussed in detail below) cannot be indicated as such because the available takeover structures are regulated by mandatory provisions of law and depend very much on whether the set thresholds are met.

Directors' Responsibilities

[329] The offering party in the course of a takeover bid is obliged to present the tender offer document (along with all accompanying documents) to the FSC. The offering party should also submit the documentation to the management body of the target company on the same day that it is submitted to the FSC. The management body of the target company, in turn, presents the tender offer to the employees' representatives or the employees themselves, if there are no employee representatives.

[330] Within seven days of receipt of the tender offer, the management body of the target company shall present a reasoned opinion on the proposed transaction to:

(i) the FSC;

(ii) the offering party; and

(iii) the employees' representatives (or, where there are no such representatives appointed, to the employees themselves).

[331] The reasoned opinion should contain among others: (i) the managemen body's position with respect to the anticipated transaction; (ii) the effects tha acceptance of the tender offer might have on the target company, its employee (iii) as well as an opinion on potential effects of the strategic plans of the offerin party for the target company and their likely consequences for the employees an the working place of the target company. The opinion should further contain info mation concerning the existence of agreements for exercising of the voting right attached to the company's shares, as long as such information is available an known to the management body, as well as information concerning the number c shares in the company held by the members of the management body thereof an whether the said members intend to accept the offer.

[332] In cases where the management body of the target company is provided wit an opinion of the employees' representatives with respect to the anticipated trans action, this opinion is attached to the management board's opinion.

[333] As a general tendency, members of management bodies in Bulgarian publi companies are appointed by the majority shareholders of such companies, there fore it is unusual for the management bodies to oppose the tender offer and issue negative opinion with respect to a proposed transaction.

[334] The POSA establishes specific prohibitions concerning the permitted activi ties of the members of the management body following the submission of the ten der offer by the offering party. The target's board is not allowed to undertake an defensive measures against the takeover.

[335] The list of prohibited activities includes:

- (i) entering into transactions that would lead to significant changes to the tar get company's property;
- (ii) issuing of new shares;
- (iii) any other activities which are aimed at frustrating the acceptance of th tender offer or which establish grounds for material difficulties or addi tional expenses.

[336] However, such actions could be validly performed after an authorisatio resolution of the target company's shareholders meeting.

[337] The explicit rules applying to the restrictions of the management body' actions do not apply in a case where the management body is trying to obtain competing tender offer.

Partial Offer

[338] Offers must be addressed to all shareholders of the target under undiscrimi nating terms. The public purchase offer may target a portion of the target's shar capital.

Mandatory Bids

[339] A mandatory takeover will need to be performed in any case if a person:

(i) has acquired directly, through related persons or indirectly over 50% of the voting shares in the general meeting of a public company;
(ii) has acquired directly, through related persons or indirectly more than two-thirds of the voting shares in the general meeting of a public company;
(iii) holds directly, through related persons or indirectly over 50% of the voting shares in the general meeting of a public company and intends to make, within a period of one year, an additional (direct or indirect) acquisition of more than 3% of the voting shares of the said public company.

[340] The mandatory bid should be performed within a fourteen-day period of the above-specified thresholds being met. The acquirer also has the rights to sell the shares within the fourteen-day period, so that as a result its shareholding falls below the established thresholds.

[341] In cases where the surpassing of the threshold was a result of a decrease in the share capital of the target company through the withdrawal of the company's own shares or reorganisation of the company, the period for the registration of the mandatory bid is one month from the registration of the respective circumstance with the Commercial Registry, where applicable.

Voluntary Bids

[342] Besides mandatory bids, the POSA also regulates so-called voluntary bids, which is a situation where the offering party is not obliged to make a bid but merely has the right to do so.

[343] In particular, the right of voluntary bid is in place in the following situations:

(i) when a person acquires directly, through related parties or indirectly more than 90% of the shares with voting rights in the general meeting of a public company;
(ii) when a person owns more than 5% of the shares with voting rights in the general meeting of a public company and wishes to acquire in addition more than one-third of the shares with voting rights in the general meeting of the public company.

Buying Shares in Advance of, or During, a Bid

[344] The offering party is generally entitled to purchase shares in the target in advance of announcing a takeover offer, as long as it does not meet the thresholds for making a mandatory bid (as specified above). Once the offering party acquires a certain number of voting shares, it could also raise a voluntary bid (as specified above).

Disclosure Obligations

[345] When a shareholder in a public company holds voting shares exceeding 50% or two-thirds of all the voting shares of the company, an obligation to make a mandatory bid is triggered.

[346] The tender offer must be performed within fourteen days of the acquisition of the shares.

[347] When calculating the shares of the particular shareholder, to the shares directly held by the shareholder are added also any shares held by related parties and indirect shareholdings.

[348] Within the meaning of the POSA, 'related parties' are those persons who, on the basis of an express or tacit, written or oral agreement with the bidder or the target company, aim to acquire control of the target company or to frustrate the successful outcome of a tender offer, as well as any persons who together with the bidder control a third party.

[349] Indirect shareholdings are shareholdings held by third parties either for the account of the major shareholder or third parties with whom the major shareholder has concluded an agreement for the common management of the company through joint voting.

[350] Further, under the provisions of the POSA, if a bidder acquires 5% or an amount that is a multiple of 5% of the voting rights in a public company, then that bidder is obliged to disclose this to the FSC and to the respective public company itself. The same disclosure obligation also applies to persons directly or indirectly holding derivatives entitling them to acquire, on their own initiative and on the grounds of a written contract, voting shares in a public company. The respective public company is obliged to disclose that the participation of a specific shareholder has exceeded the 5% barrier (or a participation multiple of 5%) to the public within a three-day period.

Exclusivity and Break Fees

[351] Exclusivity is not explicitly regulated under the POSA. Bearing in mind the general principle that all investors must be treated equally, exclusivity arrangements would most probably be treated as a violation of this principle.

[352] Break fees are also not regulated by the POSA. They are not common in the Bulgarian market.

Constraints on Due Diligence

[353] The undertaking of a due diligence of a public company is a challenging task because most of the information is treated as confidential. In most cases, public companies are unwilling to provide the offering party and its consultants with much documentation related to the company's dealings. One of the significant problems is that giving access to a data room where confidential information is uploaded contains significant risks of unauthorised disclosures. This risk could be mitigated by execution of confidentiality and non-disclosure agreements.

[354] It is common for consultants to seek and obtain publicly available information regarding the target company by conducting various searches and checks with different public registries and even the target company's website (public companies in Bulgaria are required by law to maintain a website where certain financial and business information must be uploaded in order to be disclosed to the public and the FSC).

[355] However, in privately negotiated transactions it is common for the majority shareholder to provide the bidder with extensive information enabling a due diligence to be conducted. In practical terms it is often the management body that has possession of such information (not the majority holder). Therefore the information can only be provided with the consent of the target's management body.

[356] Bidders should always take account to not breach the rules on insider trading and information contained in the Act against Market Abuse with Financial Instruments. In cases where the FSC discovers a violation of these rules, it may stop the trading in the company's shares (and/or financial instruments) for a specific period.

[357] Any information related to the bid (such as terms and conditions, prices, numbers of shares which the bidder wishes to acquire) is deemed inside information before its registration for approval with the FSC and therefore should not be disclosed to third parties.

[358] Any advertisements and publication related to the tender offer should indicate the issue number and the publication date of the national daily newspapers where the information was published. Advertisements and PR activities can take place only when the tender offer is already published in accordance with the POSA provisions.

Announcement Obligations

[359] The bidder must publish the tender offer together with the written opinion of the target's management body within a three-day period following the expiration of the term for issuing a prohibition on the takeover bid by the FSC (this information must also be presented to both employees of the bidder and the target company) in one of the national daily newspapers or on the webpage of a news agency or another media that can ensure the effective distribution of the information among the public in all Member States. This announcement is intended to provide the public with information on the takeover. Before that official announcement is procured, all information related to the takeover bid should be considered confidential and must be kept secret from third parties.

[360] In addition, the potential leakage of information should be viewed in light of the obligation of the target to protect inside information and prevent any disclosure of the information about the offer.

Minimum Price Obligations Imposed on a Buyer

[361] The method for calculating the minimum price is expressly regulated fo each type of public offer.

[362] In the case of a mandatory bid by a bidder holding over 50% or over two thirds of the votes or of voluntary bids by a bidder holding over 90% of the votes i a public company's general meeting, the price offered must be at least the highes of the following:

(i) the fair price per share, calculated according to generally accepted valua tion methods as detailed in a special ordinance;
(ii) the average market price of the shares over the previous six months prio to the registration of the bid, respectively before the date on which the reg istration obligations should have been completed, if the mandatory bid ha not been registered and this price is higher than the average market pric of the shares for the last six months prior to the bid registration;
(iii) the highest price per share at which the bidder (its related parties or asso ciated companies) has acquired shares during the six months before the bi registration. If this price cannot be calculated, the price must be equal t the latest issue price or the latest price paid by the bidder, whichever of th two is higher.

[363] For voluntary bids by a minority shareholder, as well as for mandatory bid where they exceed the 3% threshold by shareholders already holding more tha 50% of the voting rights, the price cannot be lower than the average market pric of the shares over the previous six months. Where such price cannot be calculate the bidder must offer to pay the highest price per share for which it (its related par ties or associated companies) has acquired shares during the six months before th bid registration.

[364] In compliance with the general principle of non-discrimination of share holders, the price offered must be the same for every holder of the respective clas of shares. The adequacy of the price must be supported by relevant documenta tion, which shows, among others, the methods used for the calculation of the price

[365] If until expiry of the term of the tender offer, the offering party acquire directly, through related parties or indirectly voting shares in the target company a a price higher than the one offered in the tender offer, then the offering party ha to increase the offered price to that higher price. In this case, the purchase of th shares will be affected at the higher price in respect of all shareholders who hav accepted the offer before or after the increase.

Same Terms

[366] The same terms have to be offered to all shareholders.

Conditions with Respect to the Bid

[367] As far as mandatory bids and voluntary bids by a shareholder holding more than 90% of the shares in the target company are concerned, no conditions to the tender offer are allowed.

[368] Certain conditions for voluntary bids by minority shareholders are acceptable under the POSA. A voluntary bid by such a shareholder may be conditioned by a minimum acceptance of shares (e.g., at least one-third of the voting rights). The bid could also be conditioned by the maximum number of shareholders who will accept it.

General Comments on Timetable

[369] The timeline of a public offer is outlined in the table below:

No.	*Timing*	*Action*
1.	Day 1	The day when the circumstances giving the right/obliging the bidder to make a respective type of bid have taken place.
2.	+ 14 days	Registration of the bid with the FSC. The intention/obligation of the bidder to make a bid must be announced within a 14-day period to the FSC and the CPC (if applicable).
3.	+ 7 days (as of the registration of the bid with the FSC)	On the day of the registration of the bid with the FSC, information about the bid should be submitted also to the target's management body, the bidder's employees and to the stock exchange where the target company's shares are traded (with an explicit indication that the bid is still not approved by the FSC). The target company's management body should deliver to the FSC, the bidder and its employees, its motivated position with respect to the tender offer.
4.	+ 20 days (as of the registration of the bid with the FSC)	Within this term the FSC issues its statement for approval or preliminary prohibition of the take-over
5.	+ 3 days (as of the approval of the bid by the FSC)	Within this term the bidder can publish the tender offer as described in paragraph [359].

No.	*Timing*	*Action*
6.	+ 28–70 days (as of the publication of the offer in two national newspapers)	The tender offer should contain a term for accepting the offer, which can be no less than 28 days and no longer than 70 days (unless a competing tender offer has been submitted).
7.	+ 20 days (as of the registration of the bid with the FSC)	If the FSC issues a preliminary prohibition of the tender offer it will give the bidder an additional 20-day period to amend/supplement its initial offer or to provide further information (as the case may be).
8.	The date when the term for the bid expires – publication of the result	The bid offer, along with the reasoned opinion of the target's management body, should be published in one national daily newspaper or on the webpage of a news agency or another media as described in paragraph [359] above.
9.	+ 3 days (as of the end of the bid term)	Information about the bid should be published on the websites of the target company, the investment intermediary and the stock exchange where the shares of the target company are traded.

Merger Control

[370] In cases where the acquisition of control in the public company meets the criteria for concentration listed below, a prior written approval from the CPC would also be required. A concentration takes place where the sum of the total turnovers of all undertakings participating in the concentration on the territory of the Republic of Bulgaria for the previous financial year exceeds BGN25 m (approximately EUR13 m), and:

(i) the turnover of all of the participating undertakings on the territory of the Republic of Bulgaria for the previous financial year exceeds BGN3 m (approximately EUR1.5 m); or

(ii) the turnover of the target company on the territory of the Republic of Bulgaria for the previous financial year exceeds BGN3 m (approximately EUR1.5 m).

[371] Participating undertakings are obliged to notify the CPC following the execution of the public announcement (publication) of the bid or the acquisition of control, but before any actual actions are taken for the implementation of the transaction. In exceptional cases, upon the parties' request, the CPC may assess the concentrations before the tender bid is publicly announced if the parties present sufficient evidence of their intentions to proceed to the announcement.

[372] While the decision of the CPC is pending, no actions in fact and in law related to the intended concentration are permitted. Failure to meet this prohibition would trigger administrative liability in the form of a sanction imposed on the participating undertakings. The sanction amounts to up to 10% of the aggregate turnover for the preceding financial year of the participating undertakings.

[373] The preliminary investigation on the submitted notification takes approximately twenty-five business days. During this period the CPC assesses the concentration and issues a decision for approval or denial of the concentration (for more details please *see* paragraphs [446]–[497]).

Content of Documents

[374] The offer documents are regulated materials and subject to the approval of the FSC. If the FSC determines that the documents contain insufficient information, it may request the bidder to amend/supplement them.

[375] The tender offer must contain the following information:

(i) name or company name, registered office and address of the party offering the tender and of the investment intermediary thereby authorised;
(ii) shares or class of shares, as the case may be, covered by the tender offer;
(iii) number of voting shares which the offering party does not hold and is obligated to seek or seeks to acquire;
(iv) proposed price per share (as defined according to the minimum requirements for consideration specified above);
(v) compensation for the rights of the shareholders which may be limited (i.e., limitations to voting rights) including the procedure and manner of its payment and the methods of its determination;
(vi) information concerning the types and number of shares which the offering party holds, whether directly or through connected parties, in the target company;
(vii) term for acceptance of the offer;
(viii) terms and conditions under which the offering party will finance the acquisition of the shares and proof of availability of the resources necessary for the purchase or the securities necessary for exchange (information with regard to the financing of the acquisition);
(ix) the intentions of the offering party regarding the future operation of the target company and of the offering party to the extent the latter is affected by the tender offer, including: (i) retention of the members of the management bodies and the employees of the said companies; (ii) material changes in the terms and conditions of the employment contracts; (iii) the strategic plans of the offering party for the two companies; and (iv) any possible consequences of the offer on the employees and the locations of the companies' places of business;
(x) term for the fulfilment of obligations upon acceptance of the tender offer;
(xi) applicable law to the contracts between the offering party and the shareholders upon acceptance of the tender offer and the competent court;

(xii) any other particulars and documents as may be prescribed by means of sec-ondary legislation or as may be requested by the FSC.

Withdrawal of the Bid

[376] Under the POSA withdrawal is possible only in some cases and under spe-cific circumstances.

[377] In the case of mandatory bids, the bid can be withdrawn only if: (i) the offe cannot be fulfilled due to circumstances beyond the control of the offering party (ii) the term of its acceptance has not expired; and (iii) the withdrawal wa approved by the FSC. In such case information about the withdrawal should b published in one national daily newspaper or on the webpage of a news agency o another media that can ensure the effective distribution of the information to th public in all Member States within seven days of the approval issued by the FSC.

[378] In the case of voluntary bids by a minority shareholder, the bid can be with-drawn at any time.

[379] The FSC immediately notifies the regulated market, as well as the invest-ment intermediary or the Central Depository where the documents certifying th shares have been deposited, about the withdrawal of the offer. Within three days c receipt of any such notice, the investment intermediary or the Central Depositor ensures that all certifying documents for the shares are duly returned to the share-holders who have accepted the offer.

Amendments to the Initial Offer

[380] The offering party may at any time extend the acceptance term of the offe within the maximum admissible period of seventy days. The proposed price pe share can also be increased. In such case, the purchase of shares is effected at th higher price in respect of all shareholders who have accepted the offer, whethe before or after the increase. The offering party may introduce other amendment in the offer as well, subject to prior approval by the FSC. Such amendments shoul be filed with the FSC and published without delay in one national daily newspape or on the webpage of a news agency or another media that can ensure the effectiv distribution of the information to the public in all Member States. The amend-ments are deemed approved unless the FSC issues a prohibition within three busi-ness days of submission.

When Does Control Formally Pass to the Buyer?

[381] The takeover transaction is deemed closed with the expiration of the terr specified by the bidder in the tender offer document. The purchase price must b paid within seven days of the expiration of the term.

[382] The rights attached to the shares subject of the tender offer are transferre upon registration with the Central Depositary.

Squeeze-Out and Buy-Out Procedures

Compulsory Purchase of a Minority Shareholding

[383] A bidder who, as a result of a tender offer addressed to all shareholders with voting rights, has acquired directly, indirectly or through related parties at least 95% of the voting shares in a public company has the right (within three months as of the end of the tender offer) to purchase the voting shares of the remaining shareholders. Such purchase should be approved by the FSC.

[384] The purchase price must be at least equal to the price:

(i) proposed in the tender offer whereby the threshold of 95% was reached in the course of a mandatory bid;
(ii) proposed in the tender offer whereby the threshold of 95% was reached in the course of a voluntary bid, provided that the bidder holding 95% has acquired no less than 90% of the voting shares in the said tender offer;
(iii) in all other cases – a price determined in accordance with the minimum price requirements, as specified in paragraphs [361]–[364].

[385] The FSC issues its approval within fourteen days of receipt of the offer document. Within three days of issuance of the approval, the bidder should submit the proposal to the target company and the regulated market where the shares of the company are admitted for trading. Publication in one national daily newspaper or on the webpage of a news agency or another media that can ensure the effective distribution of the information to the public in all Member States, on the target company's website as well as on the websites of the investment intermediary and the regulated market where the shares of the company are admitted for trading and notification to the employees are also required. The transfer of the shares and the payment of the price must be made simultaneously, but not later than seven business days from the publication referred to in the preceding sentence.

Buy-Outs Initiated by a Minority Shareholder

[386] Minority shareholders may also require a bidder who has acquired as a result of a tender offer directly, indirectly or through related parties at least 95% of the votes in the general meeting of a public company, the purchase of their voting shares within three months as of the end of the tender offer. The request should be in writing and should contain data about the shareholder and the shares held thereby. The procedure for the compulsory purchase of a minority shareholding applies accordingly.

[387] The purchase of the shares should be completed within thirty days of receipt of the written request.

Sanctions

[388] Breach of the relevant takeover rules constitutes an administrative offence and may result in administrative liability. Various monetary sanctions are established for different violations of the provisions of the POSA, such as:

(i) breach of the bidder's obligation to provide the target company with information about the offer simultaneously with the filing with the FSC would be punished with a fine ranging between BGN1 000 (approximately EUR500) and BGN2 000 (approximately EUR1 000);

(ii) breach of the offering party's obligation to register a tender offer with the FSC within fourteen days of execution of the agreement or after acquisition of shares would be punished with a fine ranging between BGN3 000 (approximately EUR1 500) and BGN5 000 (approximately EUR2 500);

(iii) breach of the obligation for registration of a mandatory bid or a voluntary bid would be punished with a fine ranging between BGN7 000 (approximately EUR3 500) and BGN10 000 (approximately EUR5 000).

[389] The POSA provides for higher sanctions if the respective breach is committed more than once or if a particular wrongful action has not been suspended.

[390] If intentional, a breach of certain takeover rules (e.g., those for insider trading) can also result in a criminal offence.

Other Relevant Laws and Due Diligence Issues

Anti-bribery and Anti-corruption Laws Affecting M&A Activity in Bulgaria

General Remarks

[391] For years, Bulgaria has been ranked amongst the EU Member States with the highest corruption rates. On the international level, in the 2017 Corruption Perceptions Index prepared by Transparency International, Bulgaria continues to be ranked with the lowest score among the EU Member States. However, it has climbed up the ladder by four points compared to 2016, which indicates that levels of corruption might be decreasing.

[392] There are no legal grounds that would exclude the application of the Foreign Corrupt Practices Act or the UK Bribery Act in Bulgaria.

Anti-bribery Laws in Bulgaria

[393] Under Bulgarian law, a bribe means any unjustified enrichment or transfer of direct assets or any other benefits to the bribed person or to a person of his or her choice. Regardless of whether the bribe is received directly or indirectly, the bribed person is not entitled to the benefits he or she receives.

[394] Only individuals can commit crimes of corruption in Bulgaria since criminal liability requires the presence of guilt. Consequently, a legal entity could not be held criminally liable for committing a crime in Bulgaria. However, an administrative sanction amounting up to BGN1 m (approximately EUR500 000) may be imposed on a legal entity that was enriched as a result of a corruption-related offence.

[395] The Bulgarian Criminal Code recognises the following crimes of corruption:

(i) active bribery in the public sector – an official accepts a gift or any other undue benefit, or accepts a proposal or a promise of a gift or benefit, in order to perform or to fail to perform an act related to his functions or responsibilities or because he has performed or failed to perform such an act;
(ii) passive bribery in the public sector – a person offers, promises or gives a gift or any other material benefit to an official in order to perform or not to perform an act falling within the official's functions or responsibilities or because the official has performed or has not performed such an act;
(iii) mediation for active or passive bribery in the public sector;
(iv) abuse of power – an official violates or fails to fulfil his/her duties or exceeds his/her powers or rights for the purpose of acquiring a benefit for himself/herself or for another, or to cause damage to another, from which significant harmful consequences may result;
(v) abuse of official position – an official uses his/her official position to acquire unlawful benefits for himself/herself or for another.

Money Laundering Regulations

[396] The main regulation is in the Bulgarian AML Act (promulgated in State Gazette No. 27 of 27 March 2018, last amendments promulgated in State Gazette No. 94 of 13 October 2018).

[397] The AML Act implements Directive (EU) 2015/849 of the European Parliament and of the Council of 20 May 2015 on the prevention of the use of the financial system for the purposes of money laundering and terrorist financing, amending Regulation (EU) No 648/2012 of the European Parliament and of the Council, and repealing Directive 2005/60/EC of the European Parliament and of the Council and Commission Directive 2006/70/EC.

[398] No deviations of interest are present in the Bulgarian regulation from the general legal framework on AML on an EU level.

[399] Money laundering is a crime under the Bulgarian Criminal Code and could be sanctioned by imprisonment from one to six years and a fine of between BGN3 000 and BGN5 000 (approximately EUR1 550 to EUR2 560). The sanctions are imposed cumulatively.

[400] The legal framework further includes the Measures against the Financing of Terrorism Act (promulgated in State Gazette No. 16 of 18 February 2003, as amended).

Significant Environmental or Product Safety Laws

Environmental Laws

[401] The EU is considered among the jurisdictions with the most comprehensive set of environmental legislation. As such, a great number of laws exist at both EU and national levels regulating various environmental issues, such as climate change, air quality, waste management, biological diversity, etc. As a genera approach, almost every Bulgarian act in this area implements in Bulgaria the lega framework related to a certain environmental area at the EU level. There ar hardly any significant deviations when EU acts are transposed.

[402] A non-exhaustive list of some of the most significant environmental law includes the following:

(i) Environmental Protection Act, promulgated in State Gazette No. 91 of 2 September 2002, as amended.
(ii) Clean Ambient Air Act, promulgated in State Gazette No. 45 of 28 Ma 1996, as amended.
(iii) Water Act, promulgated in State Gazette No. 67 of 27 July 1999, a amended.
(iv) Soil Act, promulgated in State Gazette No. 89 of 6 November 2007, a amended.
(v) Waste Management Act, promulgated in State Gazette No. 53 of 13 Jul 2012, as amended.
(vi) Protection from Environmental Noise Act, promulgated in State Gazett No. 74 of 13 September 2005, as amended.
(vii) Liability for Prevention and Remedying Environmental Damage Act, pro mulgated in State Gazette No. 43 of 29 April 2008, as amended.
(viii) Biological Diversity Act, promulgated in State Gazette No. 91 of 25 Sep tember 2002, as amended.
(ix) Climate Change Mitigation Act, promulgated in State Gazette No. 22 of 1 March 2014, as amended.
(x) Protection against the Harmful Impact of Chemical Substances and Mix tures Act, promulgated in State Gazette No. 10 of 4 February 2000, a amended.

[403] It is a common practice in Bulgaria to have detailed regulation of environ mental issues in secondary legal acts such as ordinances, instructions, statues.

Product Safety Laws

[404] Product liability is mainly regulated by the Consumers Protection Act (CPA (promulgated in State Gazette No. 99 of 9 December 2005, last amendments pro mulgated in State Gazette No. 37 of 4 May 2018). Manufacturers, importers and under certain circumstances, distributors and retailers, may be held liable fo defective products or products that do not comply with the sale purchase agree ment. Any contractual clause excluding or limiting consumer legal rights are nu and void. Special rules apply to certain categories of goods.

[405] Specific safety requirements are introduced in the Products Technica Requirements Act for certain products, which represent a higher risk for consum ers (promulgated in State Gazette No. 86 of 1 October 1999, last amendments pro mulgated in State Gazette No. 1 of 3 January 2019). The act sets out the genera framework, which is detailed additionally in a number of ordinances that cove specific products.

Protection and Enforcement of IPRs in Bulgaria

Registration of IPR

[406] The following Intellectual Property Rights (IPRs) are recognised in Bulgaria and are therefore subject to protection:

(i) Copyrights – any literary, artistic and scientific work resulting from a creative endeavour and expressed by any mode and in any objective form. Databases, as well as computer software, are also protected by copyrights.

(ii) Rights neighbouring to copyrights – including the rights of: performing artists over their performances; producers of phonograms over their recordings; producers over the initial recording of a film or another audio-visual work over the original copy, as well as over the copies produced as a result of this recording; radio and television organisations over their programmes;

(iii) Industrial property rights recognised in Bulgaria and, therefore, subject to protection, include:

- patents for inventions – they are registered in the Bulgarian Patent Office following an application by the inventor or his/her legal successor (detailed regulation can be found in the Patents and Utility Models Registration Act (promulgated in State Gazette No. 27 of 2 April 1993, last amendments promulgated in State Gazette No. 58 of 18 July 2017));
- utility models – they are registered in the Bulgarian Patent Office following an application by the inventor or his/her legal successor (detailed regulation can be found in the Patents and Utility Models Registration Act (promulgated in State Gazette No. 27 of 2 April 1993, last amendments promulgated in State Gazette No. 58 of 18 July 2017));
- industrial designs – they are registered in the Bulgarian Patent Office following an application by the designer (detailed regulation can be found in the Industrial Designs Act (promulgated in State Gazette No. 81 of 14 September 1999, last amendments promulgated in State Gazette No. 85 of 24 October 2017));
- trademarks – they are registered in the Bulgarian Patent Office following an application by the proprietor (detailed regulation can be found in the Marks and Geographical Indications Act (promulgated in State Gazette No. 81 of 14 September 1999, last amendments promulgated in State Gazette No. 61 of 24 July 2018));
- geographical identifications – they can be either an appellation of origin or an indication of source, and they are registered in the Bulgarian Patent Office; the right to file an application vests in any person who carries on a production activity in the specified geographical locality, provided that the goods this person produces conform to the established properties or peculiarities (detailed regulation can be found in the Marks and Geographical Indications Act (promulgated in State Gazette No. 81 of 14 September 1999, last amendments promulgated in State Gazette No. 61 of 24 July 2018));

- other – such as new plant varieties; new animal breeds; topography of integrated circuits.

[407] The Bulgarian Patent Office maintains an online registry where inquiries related to registered trademarks, geographical identifications, designs, national and European patents, utility models and even supplementary protection certificates can be made. The information is provided free of charge, in Bulgarian and in English, and without registration at: http://portal.bpo.bg. The application for registration, as well as amendments of an existing registration, can be submitted online through the portal after creating a profile.

[408] The Bulgarian Patent Office issues on a regular basis the Official Gazette of the Patent Office of the Republic of Bulgaria. The Official Gazette is published twice per month, in the middle and at the end of the month, with English translation of the table of contents. It can be used as a trustworthy source of information on verification of industrial property rights for due diligence processes. Since May 2009, the Official Gazette is issued and distributed in electronic form only and is available online on the official website of the Bulgarian Patent Office. Issues before May 2009 are available in hard copy only in the BPO's library.

Protection and Enforcement of IPR

[409] Bulgaria is a member of the World Trade Organisation (WTO) and the World International Property Organisation (WIPO). It is also a party to a number of international conventions that focus on the protection and enforcement of IPRs. There are also certain obligations that result from Bulgaria being an EU Member State in line with the applicable EU legislation.

[410] Bulgarian IPR legislation corresponds to the international standards set out in legal acts such as (the list is non-exhaustive):

(i) the Berne Convention for the Protection of Literary and Artistic Works;
(ii) the Paris Convention for the Protection of Industrial Property;
(iii) the Madrid Agreement Concerning the International Registration of Marks;
(iv) the Agreement on Trade-Related Aspects of IPRs;
(v) the Hague Agreement Concerning the International Registration of Industrial Designs.

[411] On the national level, protection and enforcement of IPRs can be sought as follows:

(i) protection by means of the criminal law – the Bulgarian Criminal Code qualifies as crimes certain violations of IPRs such as plagiarism and piracy. This is the most intense form of protection. Violations can be sanctioned by imprisonment and/or a fine;
(ii) protection by means of administrative law – every act which regulates a certain object of intellectual property, contains specific provisions on sanctions when a violation of IPR occurs. The administrative sanctions in these cases

are fines. The measures are focused on punishing the wrongdoer and ceasing the violation rather than indemnifying the holder of the title;

(iii) protection by means of civil law – acts which regulate a certain object of intellectual property provide the possibility for the holder of the title to claim damages in cases of violation by a third party of his IPR. The purpose of the claims is not only to cease the violation but also to compensate the holder for losses incurred.

[412] The existing legal framework on IPRs protection is fully synchronised with international standards for protection. However, enforcement of IPR is not always easy due to the complex nature of such disputes and the ability of courts to resolve such cases.

Agents and Distributors

[413] Agents who act as trade representatives (within the meaning of the BCA) are entitled to compensation upon termination of their contract with the principal if either of the following conditions is satisfied:

(i) the clientele of the principal was established by the trade representative and the principal continues to enjoy its benefits after the termination; or

(ii) the trade representative has significantly increased the volume of transactions concluded with the clientele of the principal.

[414] Compensation amounts to the annual commission of the trade representative, calculated on the basis the trade representative's average annual commission for the entire duration of its contract with the principal, but for no longer than the five preceding years. Compensation is payable to the heirs of the trade representative, if applicable.

[415] The trade representative is not entitled to compensation on termination if:

(i) the contract was rightfully avoided by the principal due to a breach by the trade representative; or

(ii) the contract was unilaterally terminated by the trade representative (subject to certain exceptions); or

(iii) the trade representative has transferred its legal obligations under the contract to another person, including when the principal has expressed its consent to the transfer; or

(iv) the trade representative failed to notify the principal in writing on his/her claim to the compensation in the year following the termination of the contract.

[416] Upon termination of the agency contract, the trade representative is also entitled to claim compensation for deals closed or negotiated prior to the termination.

The Use of 'Change of Control' Clauses in Bulgaria

[417] 'Change of control' clauses are commonly used in Bulgaria. There are fe well-grounded legal objections against their validity and so they are generall enforceable. A 'change of control' clause contains an obligation of the debtor t notify the creditor of the upcoming transfer. It is also a rather common approach t have an obligation to obtain the consent of the other party to share transfers c other corporate changes included in the clause.

[418] It is standard practice for 'change of control' clauses to be incorporated i banking loan arrangements. They usually enable banks to declare an event c default or a mandatory prepayment event and, therefore, require the immediat repayment of existing loans, if the bank has not consented to the transfer.

[419] 'Change of control' clauses are also used in agreements that regulate long term commercial relationships, joint ventures, etc.

The Due Diligence Process

Due Diligence

[420] Bulgaria offers attractive opportunities for investment, acquisition and bus ness partnerships.

[421] Generally, potential investors (especially foreign investors) understand tha it is advisable to engage reputable legal counsel, international or Bulgarian, t assist the investors throughout an investment process. However, one cannot say th same for the local investors who do not always run proper due diligence and ar generally not prepared in terms of transaction structuring and timing.

[422] Back in the pre-crisis era, comprehensive due diligence was often performe whenever a transaction was considered in Bulgaria. The number of full due dil gence reports has now decreased significantly, mostly due to cost reasons. Red fla due diligence covering only issues with a material impact on the transaction ar becoming ever more common.

Immovable Properties

[423] Regarding investigations into immovable properties in Bulgaria, the mos common and basic check is obtaining a Property Registry excerpt. A full title chec requires investigation of at least ten years back before the date of the due diligence and it could be a burdensome process. A reform of the Property Registry is sti ongoing and currently the checks are based on the individual owner and not on th specific land plot or building. If the property has been subject to numerous trans actions and the investor wants to perform a full property check – dating back a least ten years, this could be time consuming. Sometimes one may need to perforn numerous checks of the current owners and the individuals who have acquired th

property in the past, including by way of succession. It takes time to identify and collect the relevant documents, which in some cases are not all available for review.

[424] The choice of investigation will depend on how important the immovable property is for the contemplated transaction. We are seeing an increasing volume of real estate transactions, whereas full title checks are a must for investors unless title insurances are available for the immovable properties.

Energy and Environmental Audits

[425] Energy audits are still not common. Bulgaria has fully transposed the 2012 Energy Efficiency Directive and therefore energy audits will become mandatory for all enterprises that do not qualify as small or medium sized. Energy audits and the resulting reports would probably become part of the due diligence process and the negotiations of appropriate representations and warranties.

[426] Review of the environmental authorisations and permits, where such are important for the business, is usually part of the due diligence process.

Data Rooms

[427] Virtual data rooms are widely used. The type of data rooms used in a due diligence process very much depends on the value of the transaction. Sophisticated international companies and sellers commonly, if not always, request and accordingly set up professional electronic data rooms, while some smaller local companies sometimes use free-of-charge data rooms (e.g., Dropbox, dox.bg). Physical data rooms are common for larger projects that involve disclosure of a significant amount of confidential documentation and information.

Important Aspects

[428] The 'critical' aspects of each due diligence process mainly depend on: (i) the target's industry (e.g., banks and financial institutions, licenced utility companies); and (ii) the type of the transaction, share or asset deal. Some of the most complex legal due diligence investigations are those in real estate (especially when affected by restitution), those concerning regulated targets or businesses requiring environmental authorisations. Depending on the company and the number of employees, employment aspects could be an important part of the due diligence too. This is true especially when an automatic transfer of employment will be triggered by the transaction or a reduction in headcount is envisaged. Also, upon systematic breaches of the labour legislation or discrimination at work, the competent authorities could impose sanctions for each separate breach. For companies employing hundreds of employees this can be a real issue.

[429] The Offshore Act affects many companies, especially licenced ones – credit institutions, payment institutions, energy companies, etc. The law restricts offshore companies from directly or indirectly holding interests in local companies involved in certain businesses. Non-compliance could affect the validity of the transaction and lead to withdrawal of the target company's licence or payment of monetary sanction. In such cases investigation of the corporate structure of the purchaser is a vital part of the transaction process.

[430] Even though due diligence is substantially based on documents provided by the seller, information from public sources should not be underestimated. There is a wide range of public sources such as the Commercial Registry, Property Registry, Special Pledges Registry and others. These could provide valuable information on the target, especially when a tight deadline for due diligence does not allow undertaking the bureaucratic steps for obtaining such relevant documentation/ information from the authorities.

Avoidable Pitfalls

[431] Opting for a limited-scope due diligence that involves review of only some areas could leave legal issues undetected and hidden for the investor. Therefore, full-scope due diligence is always recommended.

[432] Organisation of the due diligence process is another key aspect. Often, gathering a full set of documents requires a lot of communication and exchange of emails. This can be avoided by good planning. In this regard, the process can be facilitated if for example the persons preparing the data room have some legal background and provide only relevant documents. Cooperation by the seller, the target and their officers is key for the due diligence process.

Representations, Warranties and Indemnities

[433] One of the purposes for the due diligence process is to provide the parties to a transaction with information necessary for drafting and negotiating the share purchase agreement, warranties and indemnities. The degree of using contractual representations, warranties and indemnities in Bulgaria depends on several factors, such as: (i) the value of the transaction; and (ii) how sophisticated the parties are (professional investors as opposed to local medium to small players). These clauses are widely used in Bulgaria, even though the case law on their enforcement/ breach is generally scarce.

[434] The main legislative act that regulates contractual relationships was adopted in 1950. It does not expressly regulate representations, warranties and indemnities.

Representations

[435] They could be linked to the Bulgarian concept of pre-contractual damages.[32] Bulgarian law recognises a clear duty to negotiate in good faith and to prevent a negotiating partner from acting to its detriment when concluding a contract.

[32] Known as the concept of '*culpa in contrahendo*' in some civil law systems.

According to law, breach of this obligation leads to claim for damages by the non-defaulting party.

Warranties

[436] As a principle, under Bulgarian law, if a party does not perform its contractual obligations, the non-defaulting party is entitled to claim: (i) specific (strict) performance and damages for delayed performance; or (ii) damages for non-performance only.[33] Specific performance is the principle and, in contrast to other jurisdictions, its application is not limited only to exceptional cases. However, having in mind the nature of such contractual covenants, specific performance might not always be possible and typically, in case of breach, courts grant damages for non-performance.

[437] Courts do not always differentiate between representations and warranties and in this regard, the use of precise contractual definitions and/or wording is advisable. Based on the principle of contractual freedom parties may agree on a specific remedy (e.g., liquidated damages, right to withdraw from the contract) for a breach of representations or warranties. This is particularly important, as sometimes it is difficult to determine what type of damages are due and to evaluate them, even with the help of an expert. In such cases, the parties might be able to negotiate a liquidated damages clause from the outset and thus to achieve some predictability.

Indemnities

[438] They are also recognised based on the principle of freedom of contract. Parties may agree on specific contractual undertakings which are not expressly defined in statute. The scarce case law indicates that indemnity clauses are enforceable and could be an effective tool for allocation of risk between vendors and buyers – e.g., in the case of ongoing tax proceedings that were disclosed to the buyer.

[439] The parties may extend, without any limitations, or may minimise or even exempt (with certain limitations provided by law) the seller's liability for breach. Under Bulgarian law it is possible to limit or exclude liability under a contract, except in the event of gross negligence or wilful misconduct.

[440] The right to rescind a contract cannot be completely excluded under Bulgarian law. However, it may be limited only to specific breaches. Another peculiarity of Bulgarian law is the statute of limitations – generally, the prescription period cannot be abridged or extended. Therefore, special consideration should be paid when drafting the conduct-of-claims procedure.

[33] There might be cases where rescission of the contract is possible, which may lead to a different type of damages.

Role of the Courts

Dispute Resolution

[441] Courts are the main dispute resolution tool in Bulgaria. The courts are ger erally neutral and do not tend to support domestic residents or companies ove foreigners, nor individuals over businesses. However, in some instances, such a consumer and employee disputes, the courts tend to lean in favour of consume and employers.

[442] The independence of the judicial system is guaranteed by the Constitutio of the Republic of Bulgaria. Courts are independent and are financially an organisationally separated from the government and the government agencie Nonetheless, the independence of the courts has been called into question fro time to time, especially in cases involving major social or political issues. The Bu garian judicial system still needs improvement in areas such as lengthy court pro ceedings, lack of funds and personnel able to deal with the increasing number c cases, concentration of most of the proceedings only in the capital city.

[443] Arbitration is also widely used, especially for complex disputes (e.g., sophi ticated share purchase agreements) as arbitrators are considered more prepared t handle complex cases. Arbitration is generally faster than normal court procee ings. In contrast to regular court proceedings, arbitration hearings are not open t the public, which sometimes makes it the preferred option. Arbitration decision are recognised and enforced in the same way as ordinary court decisions. Arbitra tion decisions are not subject to appeal but only to annulment that can be invoke only on limited grounds and within a limited time period.

[444] Mediation is also available but not very popular in Bulgaria.

Enforceability of Key Contractual Provisions

[445] Freedom of contract is a general principle of Bulgarian law and contractua provisions are enforced unless they are null and void. There are a few recent cou decisions that deal with the enforcement of warranties and indemnity clauses, th binding effect of term sheets and shareholders agreements. Yet, Bulgarian cour are not always prepared to deal with the sophisticated contractual provisions tha are often found in mergers and acquisition transaction documents. Enforcement c such provisions in Bulgarian courts can prove to be a cumbersome and time consuming process. For these reasons, in many complex transactions, arbitratio (domestic or international) is recommended as a dispute resolution tool. Some times the parties might also resort to application of a foreign law (e.g., English law if this is an option.

MERGER CONTROL

Relevant Legislation and Competent Authorities

Legislative Framework

[446] Bulgarian legislation introduces a merger control regime when a concentration arises.

[447] The CPC is the national competition authority, which is competent to review and clear concentrations in Bulgaria (in Bulgarian: ***Комисия за защита на конкуренцията***; its official website is at www.cpc.bg). The CPC is a member of the European Competition Network and the International Competition Network.

[448] The CPC is a college of seven commissioners who are appointed by the National Assembly upon nomination from political parties sitting in the parliament.

[449] The merger control regime in Bulgaria is regulated by the Competition Protection Act (promulgated in State Gazette No. 102 of 28 November 2008, last amendments promulgated in State Gazette No. 77 of 18 September 2018, effective as of 1 January 2019; hereinafter the *CPA*). The 'Guidelines on defining sanctions in cases of breach of the CPA' (in Bulgarian: ***Методика за определяне на санкциите по Закона за защита на конкуренцията***) also form part of the regulatory framework as a supplementary legal act and set out the mechanics of determining the amount of fines for, among other things, failure to notify and gun-jumping.

Competent Authorities

[450] Merger reviews are conducted by the CPC.

[451] Starting from 1 January 2019, the decisions of the CPC will be subject to subsequent control by the Administrative Court – Sofia (in Bulgarian: ***Административен съд – София област***), which will hear competition cases as a first instance of appeal. The Supreme Administrative Court (in Bulgarian: ***Върховен административен съд***) will only act as cassation instance for judgments of the Administrative Court – Sofia.

[452] A one-member panel of the Administrative Court – Sofia will hear appeals against decisions of the CPC. The judgment of this instance may be appealed in law before a three-member panel of the Supreme Administrative Court.

[453] A one-member panel is competent, depending on the factual and legal background of each case, to:

(i) declare a decision of the CPC void;
(ii) amend a decision of the CPC;
(iii) annul a decision of the CPC;
(iv) return the case to the CPC for renewed review;

(v) dismiss an appeal.

[454] When acting as a cassation instance, the Supreme Administrative Court has the same powers as those described above regarding the decision of the first instance.

Filing Obligation

[455] Mergers are subject to a mandatory filing obligation when they result in a concentration. A concentration between undertakings is deemed to arise when there is a lasting change of control because of:

(i) merger or acquisition between two or more independent undertakings; or
(ii) acquisition of direct or indirect control over undertakings or any parts thereof by one or more person/s, who already have control over at least one undertaking; or
(iii) establishment of a joint undertaking, which permanently performs all functions of an economically independent subject.

[456] There is an exhaustive list of exemptions when, subject to certain requirements, the change of control is not interpreted as a concentration for the purposes of the merger control regime. These are cases when:

(i) a credit or other financial institution or an insurance undertaking, whose activities include transactions with securities on their own or on another's account, temporarily holds securities of a certain undertaking for the purpose of reselling them;
(ii) a person acquires control in order to perform actions related to the undertaking's liquidation or insolvency proceedings;
(iii) a financial holding acquires control in order to maintain the full value of the investment.

[457] For the purposes of the merger control regime, 'control' means the acquisition of rights, execution of contracts or other courses of action, which, independently or jointly, and in view of the existing factual circumstances and applicable law, enable the exerting of decisive influence over a certain undertaking through the acquisition of:

(i) the title to, or the right to use, the undertaking's property or any part thereof;
(ii) rights, including contractual ones, which provide the opportunity for decisive influence over the membership, the voting or the resolutions of the undertaking's bodies.

[458] The CPC may be notified of the concentration immediately after the execution of a binding agreement (including a memorandum of understanding or similar), a public announcement of a tender offer or an acquisition takes place. In any case, the notification has to be made prior to the implementation of the transaction.

[459] The undertakings that are involved in the transaction must refrain from any factual or legal actions related to the transaction until the merger has been cleared by the CPC.

Scope of the Control

[460] Concentrations are subject to a mandatory pre-merger notification to the CPC when either of the following conditions are met:

(i) the combined group turnover from activities in Bulgaria in the preceding financial year of all undertakings that participate in the concentration exceeds BGN25 m (approximately EUR13 m) and the individual turnover from activities in Bulgaria of each one of at least two of the undertakings concerned exceeds BGN3 m (approximately EUR1.5 m) for the same period; or

(ii) the combined group turnover from activities in Bulgaria in the preceding financial year of all undertakings that participate in the concentration exceeds BGN25 m (approximately EUR13 m) and the turnover from activities in Bulgaria of the acquired undertaking exceeds BGN3 m (approximately EUR1.5 m) for the same period.

[461] The CPA provides detailed guidance on the calculation of the amount of the turnover of the undertakings concerned in a number of different cases.

Process/Mechanics

Notification Procedure

[462] Pre-notification is possible in Bulgaria but is rare and of little practical use.

[463] The undertaking/s that acquire/s sole or joint control file a notification with the CPC.

[464] The notification must be submitted following the conclusion of a binding agreement, the public announcement of the offering or of the acquisition of control. By way of exception, the CPC could evaluate a concentration at an earlier stage in the following situations:

(i) prior to the conclusion of a binding agreement between the undertakings concerned if they provide enough evidence supporting their intention to conclude the contract (e.g., a legally binding memorandum of understanding, term sheets, similar);

(ii) prior to the public announcement of the offer when the undertakings concerned have publicly announced their intention of making an offer.

[465] The notification is made in writing. The CPC has approved a specific ten plate of notification that contains the minimum information collected in the not fication process. The information collected covers:

(i) the participating undertakings;
(ii) the undertakings and individuals exercising control over the undertakinş concerned;
(iii) the undertakings over which the undertakings concerned exercise contro
(iv) the legal structure and purpose of the concentration;
(v) the markets in which the undertakings concerned operate;
(vi) market shares and turnover of the undertakings concerned;
(vii) information about the barriers to entry;
(viii) the principal competitors, suppliers and customers; and
(ix) arguments regarding the effects of the proposed concentration on th affected markets.

[466] Typically, the notification would also include analysis of the competitiv landscape and constraints and reasoning as to why the deal should be cleared. Suj porting documents such as financial statements, business plan, etc. also need to b provided. The notification and all supporting documents must be presented i Bulgarian or in a Bulgarian-language translation.

[467] The notification form is presented in two copies – one that contains a required information, including information which the undertakings concerne consider confidential. The other copy is a redacted version without any confider tial information included in it. This is the version that is provided to other partie in the proceedings if such are constituted and wish to review the notification.

[468] The notification needs to contain the explicit request of the undertaking concerned that the CPC grants clearance to the concentration.

[469] Post-deal notifications to the CPC are not required under the CPA. The CP is competent to initiate proceedings on its own initiative and potentially impos sanctions when a concentration was effected without preliminary clearance. Th CPC's decision to institute proceedings in such cases cannot be appealed before th Supreme Administrative Court.

Assessment of a Concentration

[470] Initial assessment of the competitive effect of a concentration takes place i the *Phase 1* stage of the review. If the initial review results in concerns that th merger may hamper competition, an in-depth review (*Phase 2*) is in principl opened at the end of Phase 1.

[471] As a matter of course, the CPC institutes proceedings within three days of fi ing of the notification or after the parties provide additional information requeste by the CPC after the initial review for completeness of the filing. Information abou the opening of Phase 1 and Phase 2 is published on the CPC website.

[472] The case is assigned to a commissioner and a case handler. The Phase 1 investigation unfolds within twenty-five business days. The period can be suspended if further information has to be provided by the undertakings. If any changes to the conditions of the concentration are proposed, an additional ten business days can be added to the initial term for the purposes of their assessment.

[473] At the end of Phase 1, the merger can be cleared, banned or sent into Phase 2. The Phase 1 decision is published on the CPC website.

[474] Phase 2 would be opened when, as a result of the assessment performed during the Phase 1 inquiry, the CPC finds that the concentration gives serious reasons for suspicion that such concentration would result in the establishment or strengthening of an existing dominant position and effective competition in the relevant market would be significantly impeded. The decision of the CPC to initiate a Phase 2 review is published on its website and it is not subject to appeal before the Supreme Administrative Court.

[475] A Phase 2 review is concluded in four months following the publication of the decision to initiate it published on the CPC website. If the case is factually and/or legally complex, the CPC could extend the review period by up to twenty-five business days. The period can be further prolonged (but no longer than fifteen business days) if measures directly related to the implementation of the concentration (the so-called remedies) are imposed. This would be the case, for example, when the remedies would preserve effective competition and restrict the negative impact of the concentration on the market affected.

[476] After sufficient evidence in Phase 2 is collected, the case handler prepares a report and presents it to the assigned commissioner who informs the Chairperson of the CPC. The Chairperson schedules a close session of the CPC during which the CPC either grants clearance or renders a ruling adopting its preliminary findings (the so-called statement of objections) about the effect of the concentration on competition.

[477] In the case of such ruling, the CPC should provide the notifying parties with at least fourteen days to present their position regarding the preliminary findings. The fourteen-day period commences on the day when the notifying parties have been informed in writing of the ruling.

[478] The notifying parties could request to be heard by the CPC in a public session before a decision on the merits of the concentration is rendered. If that happens, the hearings are executed *in camera*.

[479] Once all undertakings concerned and relevant stakeholders are heard, the CPC renders a decision. By its decision, the CPC could:

(i) clear the concentration; or
(ii) clear the concentration subject to remedies; or
(iii) prohibit the concentration.

[480] Phase 1 and Phase 2 decisions of the CPC can be appealed by the notifying parties or third interested parties (if they can prove legitimate interest) before the

Administrative Court of Sofia within the fourteen days after the relevant party has been validly informed.

[481] The CPC is competent to revoke clearance it has granted if it was based on incomplete, inaccurate, false or misleading information or when the undertakings concerned fail to implement the measures directly related to the implementation of the concentration.

Timing Implications of Obtaining Approvals

[482] Phase 1 clearance is typically obtained within approximately thirty to forty business days of filing the notification. Phase 2 clearance may take from five to six months up to nine months, depending on the complexity of the case and possible suspensions/remedies.

[483] Key to expediting clearance is to provide as complete as possible notification in the initial submission. The notification must contain a consistent analysis of the competitive dynamics on the affected markets and reasoning as to why the deal qualifies for clearance.

[484] The undertakings concerned can request from the CPC an order for admitting preliminary implementation of the clearance decision. If the request were overruled, the decision for the approval would first have to come into force in order to be enforceable, which would take another two weeks (if no further implications occur).

Deals That Are Likely to Be Refused

[485] Concentrations are cleared if they do not lead to the establishment or strengthening of a dominant position that would significantly impede effective competition in the relevant market. The analysis of whether this is the case often centres on the parties' combined market position post-merger. Typically, a merger would not raise concerns if the merging parties' combined market share does not exceed 15% in the case of horizontal tie-ups and 25% in cases of combinations between players at various vertical levels of the supply chain. The actual increment to the parties' market position also plays a role in the assessment. Deals that would typically be banned are those resulting in (near) monopoly or when the combination may harm public interests (e.g., because the expected market developments as a result of the merger may run counter to national policies in the sector).

[486] Mergers that – even though establishing or strengthening a dominant position – are aimed at modernising the relevant business activity, improving the market structures and promoting consumers' interests and where the overall positive effect outweighs the negative impact on competition in the relevant market should also be approved.

Participation of Competitors and Other Stakeholders in the Procedure

[487] In principle, competitors and other stakeholders are not parties to the proceedings before the CPC. They could request that the CPC constitute them as interested parties to the proceedings if they can prove to be directly concerned by the concentration (which – as far as we are aware – has not been admitted by the CPC before).

[488] The views of competitors and other stakeholders are taken into account by the CPC in the course of market testing. Once a notification for concentration is filed with the CPC and proceedings are initiated, information on the notified concentration is published on the CPC website. Within seven days, third parties can present information or their stance on the effect of the concentration on the affected market. The positions need to be accompanied by all evidence supporting them, if any. The CPC also contacts third parties (competitors, suppliers and customers of the merging undertakings) and requests to them information regarding the effects of the market landscape and effective competition.

[489] When Phase 2 investigations are initiated by the CPC, competitors and stakeholders can provide information or their position on the effect of the concentration on the affected market within thirty days of the publication of the decision on the opening of Phase 2 in the CPC's online register. The CPC may also contact third parties and request information.

Scope for Offering Remedies to Obtain Clearance

[490] As a matter of policy, the CPC tends to favour structural over behavioural remedies in merger cases. However, it is still to be seen how these policies are put in practice, as the authority has not to date cleared a merger with remedies.

Timing of Approvals in the Context of a Bid for a Publicly Held Company

[491] In cases of a publicly held company, the notification is due following the public announcement of the offer.

[492] The restriction that no factual or legal actions can be undertaken before clearance of the concentration is granted by the CPC would not apply to publicly held companies if:

(i) different purchasers acquire joint control over the undertaking;
(ii) the CPC was notified about the concentration immediately following public announcement of the offer and before any actions are undertaken for the execution of the acquisition; and
(iii) any voting rights of the acquiring undertaking are exercised with the sole purpose of protecting the value of its investment.

Sanctions for a Breach of the Merger Control or Other Antitrust Laws

[493] The CPA provides for administrative liability when the merger control rul are breached. The CPC is competent to impose sanctions on the undertaking cor cerned in such cases. The sanction can be up to 10% of the total annual turnove from activities in Bulgaria of the infringing undertaking in the preceding financi year.

[494] More specifically, the following breaches of the merger control rules ma trigger a fine:

(i) a concentration has been executed without the mandatory pre-merger not fication to the CPC having being made or clearance being obtained;
(ii) a concentration has been executed contrary to the conditions set out by th CPC in its clearance decision;
(iii) a concentration has been executed despite the fact that the CPC ha banned the merger;
(iv) a concentration has been executed in violation of the obligation of th undertakings to refrain from any factual or legal actions related to th transaction until the merger has been cleared by the CPC.

[495] When determining the amount of a sanction, the CPC takes into account th seriousness of the violation, its duration, and all mitigating and aggravating ci cumstances relevant for the specific case.

[496] The CPC has adopted the 'Guidelines on defining sanctions in cases c breach of the CPA', which divide violations of the merger control rules into thre groups: light, not very severe and severe. The maximum amount of the sanction for each group are set at up to 5%, 7% and 10%, respectively, of the total annu turnover from activities in Bulgaria in the preceding financial year.

[497] The guidelines further provide key points to be considered when the seriou ness of the violation is evaluated as well as examples of what can be considered mit gating and aggravating circumstances.

Anticompetitive Restraints

Non-compete and Non-solicitation Obligations

[498] Non-compete and non-solicitation obligations and ancillary restraints t vendors are common practice in cases of mergers. However, their scope and dura tion should be attuned in a way not to exceed what is necessary and proportionat for transferring the value of the business sold to the buyer.

Main Constraints Affecting Competitive Behaviour after a Deal Has Been Implemented and Relevant Competition Authorities

[499] Anticompetitive restraints should be evaluated in light of Commission Notice 2005/C 56/03 on restrictions directly related and necessary to concentrations, as the legal framework of the matter has not been developed in Bulgaria.

[500] Against this background, the CPC would usually accept that non-competition and non-solicitation clauses are justified for periods of up to three years, when the transfer of the undertaking includes the transfer of customer loyalty in the form of both goodwill and know-how. When only goodwill is included, they are justified for periods of up to two years. Non-competition clauses are not permissible when only physical assets are being transferred.

[501] As far as the geographical scope is concerned, it has to be limited to the area where the vendor has offered the relevant products or services or an area it had already invested in entering prior to the transaction.

[502] Non-compete clauses can validly bind the vendor, its subsidiaries and commercial agents.

TAXATION ASPECTS

Nature of the Tax Regime

General Comments

[503] Following the accession of Bulgaria to the EU on 1 January 2007, the Bulgarian tax system has undergone significant reforms, mainly in terms of transparency and predictability. The Bulgarian tax system is well established and has not changed dramatically during recent years. The tax system is a relatively transparent and simple one. However, the level of tax-related crime (such as tax evasion) is high. Investors generally describe Bulgaria as a tax-friendly system due to the flat-rate taxes that are predominantly in place as well as its wide network of double tax treaties. Bulgaria is among the countries with the lowest taxes in the EU and it offers excellent opportunities for companies and entrepreneurs to minimise tax.

[504] In recent years, the tax authorities have tended to enforce tax regulations more aggressively. Almost every operating enterprise is subject to a tax check or tax audit[34] by the tax authorities. The tax audits often result in the imposition of fines, which can be significant in value. For the first time in many years, in 2015 the tax authorities turned their attention to individuals as well. Tax audits of individuals

[34] Bulgarian legislation makes a distinction between tax checks and tax audits. Tax checks do not result in the establishment of tax liabilities. However, a tax check can evolve into a tax audit if there is evidence for breaches of the tax legislation, which may result in tax reassessment.

who own real estate property worth over a certain amount are considered a measure aimed at, among other things, fighting corruption at the highest levels of Bulgarian society.

Liability to Tax

Liable Persons

[505] The *CITA* regulates taxation of company profits. In connection with the accession of Bulgaria to the EU on 1 January 2007, a new CITA was adopted to meet the necessity of harmonisation of Bulgarian tax legislation with the European directives concerning direct taxation. Another reason was to make the perception and application of corporate taxation easier for the taxable persons and for the revenue administration.

[506] The definition of 'taxable person' is not consolidated under Bulgarian law and every tax act contains a distinctive definition.

[507] According to the CITA, the following are liable to tax in Bulgaria:

(i) resident legal entities;
(ii) non-resident legal entities that carry out economic activity in Bulgaria through a permanent establishment that dispose of the property of such permanent establishment or which receive income from a source inside Bulgaria;
(iii) sole traders and individuals registered as tobacco manufacturers or farmers, who determine their taxable income according to the '*ITNPA*' – for withholding tax and when they perform activities liable to taxes alternative to corporate income tax;
(iv) individual merchants within the meaning given by Article 1(3) of the BCA (individuals running a business which due to its purposes and volume should be conducted in a commercial manner) – in cases specifically listed in the ITNPA;
(v) the employers and the commissioning entities under contracts for management and control – in respect of the tax on the expenses on fringe benefits;
(vi) the National Assembly – for the tax on the additional expenses of members of the parliament.

[508] Resident legal entities within the meaning of the CITA are:

(i) legal entities incorporated under Bulgarian law; and
(ii) companies incorporated under Council Regulation (EC) No. 2157/2001, and any cooperative society incorporated under Council Regulation (EC) No. 1435/2003, which registered office is in Bulgaria and which are registered at a Bulgarian public registry.

[509] The resident legal entities are liable to taxes on income accruing from all sources inside and outside Bulgaria.

[510] Non-resident legal entities are those that do not fall within the definition of resident entities for Bulgaria. Non-resident legal entities are liable to taxes on profit earned through a permanent establishment in Bulgaria, on the income from the disposition of the property of any such permanent establishment as well as on the income accrued from a source inside Bulgaria.

[511] For withholding tax purposes, any non-resident organisationally and economically distinct business unit (trust, fund and other such), which independently carries out economic activity or performs and manages investments, will likewise be a taxable person, if the owner of the income cannot be identified.

Permanent Establishment

[512] A foreign company will form a permanent establishment for tax purposes if it:

(i) has a definite place (owned, rented or used otherwise) through which, fully or partially, an economic activity is being carried out in the country, for example: place of management; branch; representative office, registered in the country; office; chamber; studio; factory; workshop; shop; storehouse for trade; service shop; installation site; construction site; mine; quarry; drill; petrol or gas well; spring or other site for deriving natural resources;

(ii) conducts business in the country through a person authorised to conclude contracts in the name and on behalf of the foreign company (except for the activities of agents, as defined in the BCA, who have independent status);

(iii) regularly performs commercial transactions with an execution place in Bulgaria, even if the foreign person at hand has no permanent representative or definite place of business.

[513] A permanent establishment should be registered with the Bulgarian BULSTAT Registry within seven days of a foreign-based company commencing its business activity in Bulgaria. Foreign legal persons and entities operating in Bulgaria as a trustee of trusts, unit trusts or other similar entities should also be registered at the BULSTAT Registry.

[514] Permanent establishments are deemed taxable persons under the CITA. Their relevant profits that could be linked to and resulted from the permanent establishment are subject to corporate income tax in Bulgaria. Permanent establishments may also be liable for alternative tax (as regards activities subject to taxation with alternative tax) and for withholding taxes.

Main Taxes

[515] The below diagram shows the system and type of taxes currently applicable in Bulgaria:

Corporate Income Tax

[516] Corporate income tax in Bulgaria is applied at a single rate of 10%.

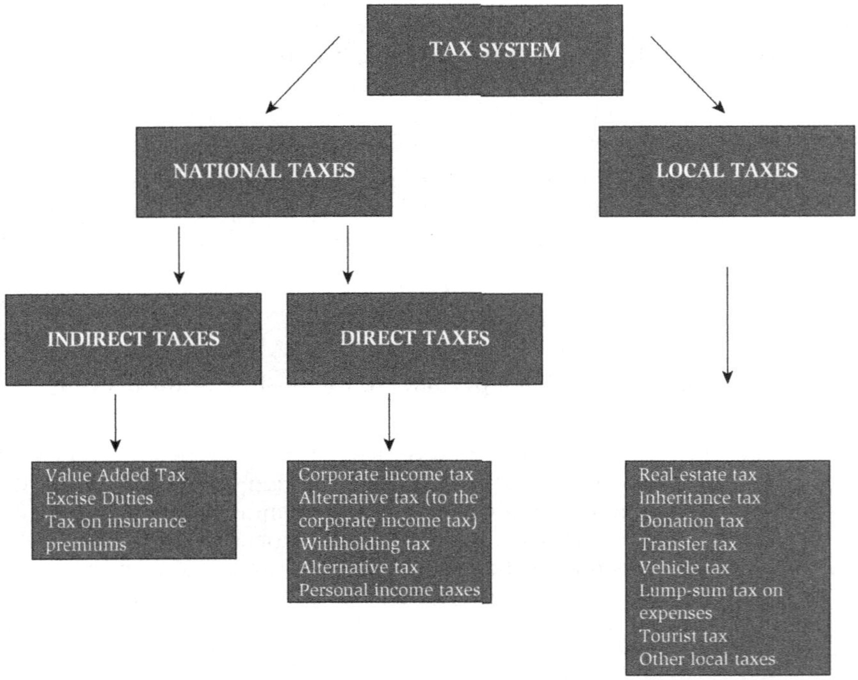

[517] Taxable persons are subject to tax on their worldwide income, no matte whether the income is generated in Bulgaria or not.

[518] Generally, the tax base for corporate income taxation is the financial resu of the respective entity (according to its income as per the annual financial state ments), which is further adjusted for corporate income tax purposes. The adjus ment is made on the grounds of items which either increase or decrease th financial result for tax purposes. Under the CITA, some expenses are permanent non-deductible for tax purposes (permanent tax differences). Other expenses ar non-deductible for tax purposes in the year when accrued for accounting purpose but could be claimed in a subsequent tax period (temporary tax differences).

[519] The permanent tax differences include, among others:

(i) costs not related to the business activity of the company;
(ii) expenses that are not substantiated with proper documents;
(iii) expenses for VAT charged in relation to items that are not tax deductible
(iv) penalties, fines and other sanctions for violation of the law;
(v) expenses classified as hidden distribution of profit;
(vi) expenses for bribery and/or concealing bribery of a local or foreign publi official;
(vii) expenses in relation to waste and shortage of inventory (unless due to forc majeure, technological losses, expiry of durability term and others);

(viii) expenses in relation to shortage of current and non-current assets (unless due to force majeure, certain amount of shortage of goods in commercial outlets with direct physical access of the customers to the merchandise);
(ix) expenses for travel and accommodation of shareholders or partners when made by individuals in their capacity of shareholders/partners.

[520] The following expenses qualify, among others, as temporary tax differences:

(i) revenue and/or expenses in relation to subsequent revaluation/impairment of assets. These are taxable, or tax deductible, in the year when the respective asset is disposed of or written off;
(ii) expenses in relation to provisions for payables or unused annual leave of employees (including salaries and social security and health insurance contributions). These expenses are tax deductible in the year when the payable is settled or when the employees effectively use their paid leave;
(iii) interest expenses exceeding the threshold established by the thin capitalisation rule (for more information please see the 'Thin capitalisation' Section below).

Alternative Tax

[521] Alternative taxes substitute the corporate income tax. They apply to three groups of taxpayers, as follows:

(i) companies engaged in gambling activities – the tax rate is 15%. The tax is final and is payable monthly;
(ii) budget enterprises – the common tax rate is 3%; however, a decreased tax rate of 2% applies for municipalities. The tax base for budget enterprises is calculated on their income from trading activities, as well as on their income from renting real estate property. The tax is final and is payable by 31 March of the year following the end of the financial year;
(iii) companies engaged in ship management – such companies can choose whether to pay corporate income tax or an alternative tax. The alternative tax rate is 10% and is calculated on the net tonnage of the ship and the number of the days in operation. The tax is payable by 31 March of the following year.

Tax on Capital Gains

[522] Capital gains derived by Bulgarian entities are included in their profits and are, in principle, subject to the 10% corporate income tax.

[523] There are, however, certain cases where capital gains are not subject to tax, among others:

(i) capital gains realised from the sale of shares in collective investment schemes and national investment funds, shares, rights and sovereign bonds traded on a regulated market within the meaning of the Bulgarian Markets in Financial Instruments Act;

(ii) transactions with financial instruments according to the procedure for repurchase or redemption by collective investment schemes which have been admitted to public offering in Bulgaria or in another EU/EEA Member State;
(iii) transactions with financial instruments according to the procedure for redemption by national investment funds which have been admitted to public offering in Bulgaria;
(iv) transactions with financial instruments according to the procedure for tender offering under the POSA or transactions of a similar type in another EU/EEA Member State;
(v) capital gains realised by non-resident taxpayers from the sale of real estate property located in Bulgaria or from the sale of shares, securities and other long-term financial assets derived from a source in Bulgaria (a 10% withholding tax would be applicable for them), etc.

Lump Sum Tax on Expenses

[524] A 10% tax on expenses is levied on the following expenses, supported by the relevant documents:

(i) business entertainment expenses;
(ii) expenses on fringe benefits provided in kind to employees and directors; the expenses on fringe benefits provided in kind further include: (a) the expenses on contributions (premiums) for supplementary voluntary social insurance, for voluntary health insurance and for life assurance (exceeding an amount of BGN60 (approximately EUR30) for each hired person); and (b) the expenses on food vouchers (exceeding an amount of BGN60 (approximately EUR30) for each hired person);
(iii) expenses related to the operation of a means of transport where used to service management operations.

[525] The lump sum tax on expenses is paid on an annual basis and is recognised as a tax deductible expense.

VAT or Sales Taxes or Other Taxes on Revenue/Sales

[526] The Bulgarian VAT Act implements Directive 2006/112/EC.

[527] The standard Bulgarian VAT rate is 20%. It applies to the supply of goods and services with a place of supply in Bulgaria, intra-Community acquisitions of goods, and imports of goods into Bulgaria.

[528] Reduced VAT rates (9% and 0%) apply to deliveries of certain goods or services.

[529] The reduced 9% VAT rate applies to accommodation in hotels, sheltered housing and other places for accommodation.

[530] The reduced 0% VAT rate applies to specific supplies, such as: (i) international transport of passengers and goods; (ii) certain supplies related to international transport; (iii) intra-Community supplies of goods; (iv) exports of goods to customers outside the EU; (v) supplies of non-Community goods places under a special customs regime; (vi) imports related services when their value is included in the custom's rate; (vii) services rendered by agents, brokers and other intermediaries acting in the name and on behalf of a third person in relation to certain export transactions.

Stamp Duties or Other Taxes on Land Transactions

[531] There are no stamp duties in Bulgaria. However, in order to be valid, land transactions have to be executed as notarial deeds, and respective notarial fees are due.

Local Taxes

[532] The Bulgarian Local Taxes and Fees Act provides for a number of local taxes which amount is defined by the municipal council in every municipality. The tax rates may differ from one municipality to another. The municipal council determines the amount of the taxes within the range established by the law.

[533] Some of the most important municipal taxes applicable to businesses include:

(a) Real Estate Tax

Taxable properties are built up land and non-built construction plots. Agricultural land tracts and forests are tax exempt. However, developed land in respect of the actually developed surface area and the adjoining ground will also be subject to tax.

The taxable persons are the owners or holders of real rights (e.g., persons using the real estate) over the taxable property.

The municipal council determines the amount of the tax within a range of 0.1%–4.5% per mil of the tax-assessed value of the real estate. A reduction of 50% of the due tax is available if the real estate property is the taxpayer's main residence.

(b) Vehicle Tax

A vehicle tax is payable by the owners of road vehicles, ships and airplanes registered in Bulgaria. The tax rate depends on the type and the characteristics of the respective vehicle (e.g., the vehicle tax for cars is determined by the engine power).

(c) Transfer Taxes

A transfer tax is levied on any real estate properties, any rights related to real estate properties or motor vehicles acquired by donation or for a consideration. The tax must be paid by the transferee of the property or by the transferor if the transferee is abroad.

The tax rate is between 0.1% and 3% of the assessed value of the transferred prop erty if the transfer is against a consideration. Donations and disposals without consideration are subject to tax at the following rates:

(i) a tax ranging from 0.4% to 0.8% is applicable to donations between sibling and the children of siblings;
(ii) a tax ranging from 3.3% to 6.6% is applicable to donations between an other persons.

The law provides for certain exemptions from transfer taxes, such as privatisatio of assets, in-kind contribution of assets to the share capital of a company.

(d) Other local taxes

Under the Local Taxes and Fees Act, the municipalities also collect some servic charges for performance or maintenance of public services such as waste collectio charge, tourist charge, and charges for various administrative services.

Capital Duties or Other Duties on Share Capital

[534] No capital duties/other duties on share capital are applicable in Bulgaria.

Business Rates

[535] No business rates are applicable in Bulgaria.

Tax on Insurance Premiums

[536] Tax on 'insurance premiums' was introduced into the Bulgarian tax syster on 1 January 2011. The tax on insurance premiums is levied on insurance prem ums under taxable insurance contracts, the risks of which are assumed by insurers The law prescribes for certain exemptions, such as insurance premiums under rein surance and retrocession contracts, life insurance and annuities, marriage an birth insurance, life insurance linked to an investment fund.

[537] Taxable persons are:

(i) insurers registered as joint-stock companies, a cooperative society or a insurer from a third state through a branch, which has received a licenc under the terms, conditions, and procedure specified in the Insuranc Code;
(ii) insurers from another EU Member State which provide services in Bulgari through exercising their right of establishment or of the freedom to pro vide services;
(iii) tax representatives – if such tax representatives have been determined i line with the procedure specified in the law.

[538] The tax base is the insurance premium received by the insurer under the tax able insurance contract. If the insurance premium is paid-in instalments, the ta base will be the part of the insurance premium received by the insurer. The tax rat is 2%.

Taxes Imposed on Employers (e.g., PAYE and Social Security Obligations)

[539] As a general rule, employment income realised in Bulgaria is subject to personal income tax and social contributions.

[540] The personal income tax is levied on the base of the employment income, at a flat rate of 10%. The employer is responsible for withholding the tax on the basis of the monthly employment remuneration.

[541] The social contributions rates are due by both the employers and the employees in different proportions, depending on the fund to which contributions are made. For the general illness and maternity fund, the unemployment fund and the health insurance fund the contributions are in the ratio 60:40 (employer: employee).

Customs

[542] Following the accession of Bulgaria to the EU, Community goods circulate freely between Bulgaria and other EU Member State without any customs payment obligations. Non-EU goods (those that are imported in Bulgaria from non-EU countries) are subject to customs duties in compliance with the EU Common Customs Tariff. Customs duties are expressed as a percentage applied to the customs value or as a fixed amount applied to a specific quantity.

Excise Duties

[543] Excise duty in Bulgaria is charged on:

(i) tobacco products;
(ii) alcohol and alcoholic beverages; and
(iii) energy products and electricity.

[544] Excise duty rates are charged as a flat amount per unit (based on the weight, volume, quantity or number of pieces) of the product upon importation or release for consumption.

[545] Exports are exempt from excise duties. Where excise duties have been paid for products that are subsequently exported, a refund can be received. Where excise duties are charged on raw materials with a content of alcohol, which have been used for production of non-dutiable food products or medicines, a refund, can be claimed also for the duties paid on the raw materials.

[546] The production of some excise goods (e.g., tobacco products, alcohol) may be carried only in fiscally controlled warehouses. Excise goods may be imported, processed and stored in fiscally controlled warehouses, as well as transported under a deferred-payment regime.

Tax Consolidation: Group Relief of Gains and Losses

Use of Gains or Losses of the Target Company Elsewhere within the Purchaser's Group

[547] Bulgarian law does not regulate tax consolidation or group taxation rules. Bulgarian companies must keep their tax accounting separately. Group members file separate tax returns and the losses incurred by a group member cannot be offset against profits made by other group members.

Controlled Foreign Company Rules

[548] Controlled Foreign Company (CFC) rules are effective in Bulgaria as of 1 January 2019, following amendments made to the CITA which implement Council Directive (EU) 2016/1164 of 12 July 2016 laying down rules against tax avoidance practices that directly affect the functioning of the internal market into the Bulgarian legislation. Pursuant to the CFC rules, additional amount of corporate tax may be due by taxpayers in Bulgaria (controlling entities) by virtue of increasing their tax financial result on the basis of either the profit or certain type of income of the CFC controlled by the taxpayers in Bulgaria. The CFC rules apply in case:

(i) the respective CFC is not being taxed, or is being taxed under a too low rate in the jurisdiction, in which it is a local taxpayer; and
(ii) certain statutory set thresholds regarding the amount of tax actually paid by the CFC and the shareholding of the controlling entity in the CFC have been reached.

[549] It should be noted that within the meaning of CITA, a CFC means not only a company but also a legal entity, another type of legal organisation, as well as permanent establishment outside Bulgaria.

[550] In accordance with the CFC rules, the tax financial result of the controlling entity will be increased by a commensurate amount of the tax profit of the CFC determined pursuant to CITA. On the other hand, in case of tax loss of the CFC, it shall not be included in the controlling entity's tax result but will be carried forward in the next five years against the same CFC's tax profit or against the tax profit of another CFC in the jurisdiction of the CFC with a tax loss.

[551] In order to avoid double taxation upon application of the CFC rules, CITA provides options to trigger:

(i) right of a tax credit of the controlling entity for certain taxes paid by the CFC; or
(ii) reduction of the tax financial result of the controlling entity;

subject to the rules specified in CITA.

CITA introduces two types of exceptions from the application of the CFC rules, namely when the CFC is exempted from corporate tax (e.g., in case the CFC should pay alternative tax in its country of tax residence) or the CFC pursues considerable business activities by using staff, equipment, assets and premises.

In relation to the application of the CFC rules, the controlling entity should keep a register of its CFC, which should include, among others, up to date details on its shareholding in the CFC and certain profit parameters of the CFC. Failure to keep the register may result in imposing a sanction on the controlling entity in an amount ranging between BGN3 000 (approximately EUR1 500) and BGN5 000 (approximately EUR2 500). In case of repeated breach, the sanction ranges between BGN6 000 (approximately EUR3 000) and BGN10 000 (approximately EUR5 000).

Tax Considerations Arising from M&A Transactions

Main Tax Issues Related to M&A Transactions

Sale of Shares (for Cash, Shares or Other Securities)

[552] See paragraph [547] above.

(a) Corporate income tax

In Bulgaria, there are no specific rules on determining the taxable amount of capital gains and losses, and they basically follow the recognition and measurement criteria under the applicable accounting framework.

The Bulgarian tax rules do not differentiate between trading profits, finance income and capital gains. As part of the accounting result, together they form the current year taxable base subject to 10% tax, unless any item is explicitly treated as a permanent or temporary tax difference.

A company should therefore include in its taxable result for the year, the sale of any shares and any capital gains/losses realised upon the transfer.

Based on the generally accepted international tax rules, gains derived from the alienation of shares may be exempt from tax in the source state, i.e., where the investment is based.

(b) VAT

The sale of shares will be regarded as a VAT-exempt supply and no VAT will be charged on the price. All historic VAT liabilities of the company will remain at the company following the transfer of the shares.

Sale of Assets

[553] Under Bulgarian law, there are two distinct types of asset deal: (i) a sale of specifically designated assets; and (ii) a sale of a going concern or a part thereto, as a pool of assets, liabilities and factual relations.

Sale of Distinct Assets

[554]

(a) Corporate income tax

If separate assets are purchased, the purchaser may acquire the assets with a ste up in their cost base and may reduce the capital gains charge on future dispos (e.g., may claim higher deductions from the sale price in the event of a future sal of assets). Tax depreciation on the tangible assets or amortisation of intangib assets may be claimed based on a higher depreciable base. All historic corporat income tax liabilities will be left with the seller.

(b) VAT

An asset purchase will be subject to the standard Bulgarian VAT rate of 20%. Th seller should charge VAT on the price of the sold assets. The purchaser should b able to recover it (if it is registered for VAT purposes in Bulgaria) if it uses th acquired assets for supplies subject to VAT (i.e., the provision of services which a not VAT exempt). All historic VAT liabilities related to the transferred assets wi remain with the seller.

Sale of Going Concern (or a Part of It)

[555]

(a) Corporate income tax

In the case of transfer of a going concern, the purchaser will have to account th acquisition as a business combination pursuant to the applicable accounting sta dards. All acquired assets and liabilities should be reported at their fair value as a the acquisition date. The difference between the acquisition cost and the fair valu of acquired assets and liabilities should be reported as goodwill. As a result, th purchaser may report the assets at their fair value and reduce the capital gain charge on a future disposal. The purchaser may claim tax depreciation on the ta gible assets or amortisation of intangible assets based on their fair value. Goodwi is, however, not tax depreciable under Bulgarian law and any expenses fro impairment or write-off of goodwill are not tax deductible. Upon transfer of th entire going concern, the purchaser assumes all historic corporate income ta liabilities.

(b) VAT

The transfer of a going concern is not regarded as a taxable supply under the Bu garian VAT Act and no VAT will be charged on the going concern purchase pric The purchaser will acquire all VAT related rights of the seller in respect to th transferred assets, including the right of VAT deductions. It will assume all VA related obligations of the seller in respect to the transferred assets, including th obligation for adjustment of utilised input VAT deductions. If the purchaser is not VAT registered, it needs to register within one week of the transfer being registered with the Commercial Registry.

Risk of Re-qualification

[556] The proper structuring of the asset deal is important as in the event of a tax audit, a sale of distinct assets may be reclassified as the sale of a going concern and vice versa by the tax authorities. In some cases where employees or know-how are transferred, or where there is no business left with the seller, the risk of reclassification of an asset deal as transfer of going concern is particularly high.

[557] The consequences of re-qualification of an asset deal as a transfer of a going concern would be a denial of the input VAT recovery. Such input VAT would thus become a cost for the seller.

Negotiation of Values

[558] As a rule, values are freely negotiable between parties. However, transactions between related parties must be at arm's length. Otherwise, the Bulgarian tax authorities may adjust the taxpayer's revenues or expenses to reflect the market value of a relevant transaction. In the case of a public company, the specific rules on price determination established in the POSA should be applied.

Carry Forward of Losses

[559] Companies are allowed to carry forward fiscal losses declared in the annual profit tax returns for a period of up to five years.

[560] Non-resident legal entities may carry forward losses attributable to their permanent establishment in Bulgaria.

Deferred Payments, Retentions, Holdbacks and 'Earn-Outs'

[561] Deferred payments, retentions, holdbacks and 'earn-outs' are generally accepted and used in Bulgaria as a means of mitigating transaction risks.

[562] Pursuant to applicable Bulgarian tax regulations, the tax on capital gains derived from transfers of assets/shares is calculated in consideration of the entire price paid or expected to be paid pursuant to the transaction documents, regardless of whether the full transaction price is paid-in one instalment or whether certain deferred payments, retentions or holdbacks apply in relation to the transaction price.

Deductibility of Acquisition Expenses as a Business Expense

[563] The deductibility of a specific expense depends very much on the accounting of such expense. Where the accounting rules state that the cost must be included in the value of the purchased asset, the company will not record an expense at the moment of the acquisition.

[564] As a result, the expense will be recognised during the asset's useful life through depreciation (in the case of fixed assets) or at the moment when the asset will leave the company's patrimony. The deductibility will be established according to the specific fiscal rules of the expense and the economic substance of the event.

Structuring the Investment

Withholding Taxes

[565] In Bulgaria, certain business and investment income of non-resident legal entities earned from sources in Bulgaria are subject to flat final income tax, which is normally levied by means of withholding. The tax rate is 10% (5% for dividend distribution and liquidation quotas).

[566] It should be noted that certain reduced rates or an exemption can be applied under the double tax treaties to which Bulgaria is a party.

[567] The following income of non-resident legal entities are subject to withholding tax:

- (i) dividends and shares in a liquidation quota, distributed by a resident legal entity in favour of:
  - (a) non-resident legal persons, excluding dividends accrued to a non-resident legal person through a permanent establishment in the country;
  - (b) resident, legal persons which are not merchants, including any municipalities.
- (ii) income with their source inside the country, distributed to a non-resident legal person, which is not accrued through a permanent establishment:
  - (a) income from transactions with financial assets and from financial assets issued by resident legal persons, the Bulgarian state and municipalities;
  - (b) interest payments, including interest within payments under a financial lease contract;
  - (c) income from rent or other provision for use of movable property;
  - (d) copyright and licence royalties;
  - (e) technical assistance fees;
  - (f) payments received under franchising agreements and factoring contracts;
  - (g) compensation for management or control of a Bulgarian legal person;
  - (h) income from agriculture, forestry, hunting ground management and fisheries within the territory of the country shall have its source inside the country;

(i) income from rent or other provision for use of immovable property, located in the country;
(j) income from disposition of immovable property, located in the country;
(k) penalties and indemnities of any kind, excluding benefits under insurance policies, charged by resident legal persons, resident sole traders or non-resident legal persons and sole traders through a permanent establishment or a fixed base in the country in favour of non-resident legal persons established in preferential tax treatment jurisdictions will be income having its source inside the country.

[568] No withholding tax is due on income from interest and royalties when accrued to associated companies which are tax resident in an EU Member State, and on dividends and liquidation quotas, distributed by local undertakings to companies which are tax resident in an EU/EEA Member State.

[569] The tax is withheld by the resident legal persons, sole traders or permanent establishments in the country which charge the income to the non-resident legal persons. An exception is the income from transactions with financial assets and the income from transactions with immovable property, including an undivided interest or a limited property right to any immovable property located in the country, where the tax is withheld from the recipient of the income.

[570] This is also the case where the payer of the income is not a taxable person under the CITA.

[571] Income from the disposition of shares in public companies, negotiable rights attached to shares in public companies, and shares and units of collective investment schemes, does not attract a tax withheld at source, if the said disposition is effected on a regulated Bulgarian securities market.

Double Tax Treaties

[572] Bulgaria has concluded more than sixty double tax treaties which provide for tax relief or a reduced tax rate.

[573] In order to benefit from the reliefs in a double tax treaty, a non-resident person has to submit an application to the tax authorities showing that this person:

(i) is a resident of the respective state, party to the double tax treaty (within the meaning given by the relevant treaty);
(ii) realises income from a source inside the Republic of Bulgaria;
(iii) does not have a permanent establishment or a fixed base within the territory of the Republic of Bulgaria, whereto the income is effectively connected;
(iv) fulfils the special requirements for application of the treaty or separate provisions thereof in respect of persons specified in the treaty itself, where such special requirements are included in the relevant treaty.

[574] The application should be accompanied by written evidence on the type, th amount and the grounds for realisation of the relevant income.

[575] The tax authorities examine the application and decide whether the doubl tax treaty could be applied in the case at hand. Once the examination is conductec the tax authorities issue an opinion on the existence or non-existence of grounc for application of the tax treaty within sixty days of submission of the initial appl cation. If the tax authority does not issue an explicit statement within the pr scribed time frame, it is presumed that there are sufficient grounds for applicatio of the double tax treaty.

[576] With respect to the application of double tax treaties in Bulgaria, a ruling c the European Court of Justice (ECJ) was delivered on 25 July 2018 (Case C-553/1 *TTL EOOD v. Direktor na Direktsia 'Obzhalvane i danachno-osiguritelna praktika' – Sofia*). The ruling deals with the situation where a local person performs transac tions with a foreign person registered in an EU/EEA country. In such case the loc person makes a payment to the foreign person, which normally is subject to a with holding tax unless a double tax treaty provides otherwise. In accordance with Bu garian law, the tax authorities have been charging the local entity wit irrecoverable default interest from the period of the due date for payment of th withholding tax until an explicit or tacit confirmation of the application of the re evant double tax treaty. The ECJ has ruled that such a regime is not compatibl with EU law.

[577] A non-resident person is entitled to appeal the refusal of the revenu authorities to allow direct application of the tax treaty.

Thin Capitalisation

[578] According to the CITA, thin capitalisation is a situation where a company (limited liability or a JSC) is excessively financed through debt rather than throug equity. If the debt-equity ratio of the company (averaged between the beginnin and the end of the year) exceeds 3:1, then a portion of the net interest expenses c the company (i.e., interest expenses less interest income) will not be tax deductible

[579] In such case the amount of non-deductible tax will be the net interes expenses exceeding 75% of the Earnings Before Interest and Taxes (EBIT). If EBI is negative, the interest expenses are tax deductible up to the amount of the inte est income of the company, if any. The non-deductible interest expenses may b deducted in a subsequent year (after deducting the interest expenses for the pa ticular year) provided that all other conditions for allowing tax interest deduction are met. Interest expenses arising from bank loans/financial leases (unless th bank/the lessor is a related party or the loan/the lease is guaranteed, secured o extended by the order of a related party), penalty interest, interest costs booked i the value of assets or tax disallowed interest expenses are not subject to thin cap talisation restrictions.

[580] As of 1 January 2019 a separate regime applies to companies with net expenses for interests exceeding the BGN value of EUR3 m, in accordance with the official exchange rate. Pursuant to the this regime, such companies should either (i) deduct for tax purposes interest expenses in an amount up to 30% of the Earnings Before Interest, Taxes, Depreciation and Amortization (EBITDA) or (ii) apply the regime described above in paragraph [576], whichever of the two options is less favourable for such companies.

Transfer Pricing

[581] Bulgarian tax law requires that transactions between a company and its related parties be carried out at arm's length. If the prices charged in such transactions (including interest on related parties loans) are not set at arm's length the Bulgarian tax authorities may, in a tax audit, for tax purposes adjust the prices to market levels.

[582] When the parent or a person related to the parent charges a subsidiary, and such charges (including interest on loans) are found by the tax authorities to exceed the market levels, the excess amount may be deemed a 'hidden profit distribution'. Interest expenses reported by the company may be deemed a hidden profit distribution by the tax authorities if at least three of the following conditions are met:

(i) the loan exceeds the equity of the borrower as of 31 December of the previous year;
(ii) the repayment of the loan or the interest is not limited by a deadline;
(iii) the repayment of the loan or the interest or the amount of the interest depends on the existence or amount of the profits of the borrower;
(iv) the repayment of the loan is subordinated to the satisfaction of other creditors or to the payment of dividends.

[583] It should be noted that the amount of the expenses qualified as hidden profits distribution is:

(i) tax non-deductible;
(ii) subject to 10% Bulgarian withholding tax on dividends if accrued to a foreign tax resident; and
(iii) subject to an administrative penalty of 20% of the amount.

[584] The Organisation for Economic Co-operation and Development (OECD) transfer pricing guidelines have not been officially adopted in Bulgaria. However, in practical terms, the Bulgarian transfer pricing methods are, to a great extent, similar to the OECD ones.

Under Bulgarian law, the taxpayer has to prove that the transaction is on an arm's length terms, and provide respective documentation supporting this statement, rather than the tax authorities.

[585] A procedure to amend the Tax and Social Insurance Procedure Code was initiated in late 2018. The amendments contemplate, among others, the introduction of rules for preparing transfer pricing documentation evidencing the arm's length basis of related-party transactions.

[586] Pursuant to the envisaged amendments, transfer pricing documentation should be prepared by:

(i) local legal entities;
(ii) foreign legal entities with permanent establishment in the country; and
(iii) certain sole traders.

[587] The obligation to prepare the documentation arises when the taxpayer:

(i) has an annual net revenue exceeding BGN16 m (approximately EUR8 m) or assets with a balance sheet value exceeding BGN8 m (approximately EUR4 m), and
(ii) is engaged in related-party transactions exceeding the statutory determined annual thresholds.

[588] A financial sanction for failure to prepare transfer pricing documentation will be introduced. The amount of the sanction would be up to 1% of the value of the related-party transaction that should have been documented.

[589] The procedure is in a rather early stage of development, as public consultations were completed in early December 2018.

EMPLOYMENT CONSIDERATIONS

Legislative Framework

Main Legislative Acts

[590] The subject matter of labour law is codified in the Bulgarian Labour Code.[35] However, numerous acts of secondary legislation also exist.

[591] Other important legislative acts are:

(i) Health and Safety at Work Act.[36]
(ii) Settlement of Collective Labour Disputes Act.[37]
(iii) Act on Information and Consultation of Workers and Employees in Community-Scale Undertakings, Groups of Undertakings and European Companies.[38]
(iv) Ordinance on the Working Time, Rest Breaks and Leaves.[39]

[35] Promulgated in SG No. 26 from 1 Apr. 1986 and SG No. 27 from 4 Apr. 1986, as amended and supplemented from time to time.
[36] Promulgated in SG No. 124 from 23 Dec. 1997, as amended and supplemented from time to time.
[37] Promulgated in SG No. 21 from 13 Mar. 1990, as amended and supplemented from time to time.
[38] Promulgated in SG No. 57 from 14 Jul. 2006, as amended and supplemented from time to time.
[39] Promulgated in SG No. 6 from 23 Jan. 1987, as amended and supplemented from time to time.

(v) Ordinance on Structure and Organisation of Wages.[40]

Employment Protection

Employment Continuity on Business Transfers

[592] Bulgaria has fully transposed the Acquired Rights Directive[41] into its Labour Code. Upon a relevant transfer, the employment transfers automatically to the new employer by operation of law. Generally, the purchaser of a business is not able to pre-select the employees it wishes to keep and those it wishes to dispense with (no cherry picking). The purchaser has to provide the same working conditions as the former employer.

[593] Bulgarian law considers all types of mergers, spin-offs, transfer of an undertaking or part of an undertaking as relevant transfers. A service provision change, including transfer of assets, may also qualify as a relevant transfer.

[594] Upon transfer of a Bulgarian business the assessment of whether the transfer is a relevant one falls under the jurisdiction of the competent Bulgarian court. However, judges have to consider the criteria for interpretation set out by the established case law of the ECJ.

Management Representation of Employees

[595] Generally, Bulgarian law does not provide for mandatory participation of employees in the company's management bodies. Limited liability companies and joint-stock companies with more than fifty employees should have an employee representative at the general meetings if the employees have elected such representative. The employees' representative should be heard before the general meeting can take decisions concerning labour and social security issues.

Information and Consultation: Obligation upon a Share Transfer or Sale of a Business

[596] A transfer of shares does not trigger any information or consultation obligations as the employer (the legal entity) would remain the same, only its shareholders would change.

[597] An information on a contemplated change of employer should be provided to the trade union and to the employee representatives (if such exist) prior to the employment transfer. This obligation applies to both the former employer and the new employer. The information obligation should be fulfilled at least two months

[40] Promulgated in SG No. 9 from 26 Jan. 2007, as amended and supplemented from time to time.

[41] Council Directive 2001/23/EC of 12 Mar. 2001 on the approximation of the laws of the Member States relating to the safeguarding of employees' rights in the event of transfers of undertakings, businesses or parts of undertakings or businesses.

prior to the relevant transfer. If the employer[42] envisages measures that woul affect the transferring employees after the transaction, consultations should also b conducted with the employees.

[598] Employees cannot prevent the transaction. However, they can terminat their employment contracts without notice if the labour conditions with the ne employer deviate adversely after the transaction.

[599] A failure to provide information or to conduct consultations cannot bloc the transaction or reflect on its validity. In such cases, the employer may fac administrative sanctions for breach of the employment legislation.

Employees' Representatives and Trade Unions

[600] There are different levels of employee representation. Bulgarian law recog nises:

(i) a general meeting of employees that can elect employee representatives;
(ii) employee representatives for information and consultation purposes; an
(iii) trade unions.

[601] Trade unions can be established at different levels – the company, industr sector or national level. One of the most important rights of trade unions is to pr cure negotiations for a collective bargaining agreement.

[602] The employment legislation in Bulgaria is generally protective towarc employees and as such provides certain rights to trade unions. Some trade unio officials enjoy special protection against dismissal. Trade unions can also represer employees before competent courts and make procedural motions on an emplo ee's behalf.

[603] However, trade unions have little power to interfere in the management decisions or block them. Therefore their rights cannot be classified as very stron

Information and Consultation: Other Instances

[604] In addition to relevant transfers, there are also other instances wher employees have to be informed and/or consulted. These include, among other cases:

(i) of mass redundancies;
(ii) when there is a recent or probable development of the employer's activiti and its economic situation;
(iii) when there are changes to the situation, structure and probable develop ments in terms of employment, especially in the case of threat to emplo ment;
(iv) when the employer plans to use or is using employees provided by a ten porary work agency;

[42] Could apply both to the former or the prospective employer.

(v) when the employer plans significant changes to the work organisation.

[605] Generally, employees cannot block the contemplated changes or developments.

Waiver of Employment Rights

[606] According to the Labour Code, a waiver of labour rights is null and void. This does not necessarily mean that the parties to an employment agreement cannot reach a post-termination settlement. But the waiver of future rights is in any case unenforceable. Considering also that Bulgarian employment law is employee protectionist, it is not possible to contract out the protection provided by law.

[607] There might be some room for manoeuvring as regards information and consultation procedures with the employees' representatives. The employer and the employees' representatives can reach an agreement on some aspects of the procedures such as the content of the provided information and the timeframe for this, the terms and subject matter of consultations. Nevertheless, this cannot be directly aimed at derogation of employees' rights.

Termination of Employment Agreements

[608] Termination of individual employment contracts is possible only on limited grounds and follows the procedures set out by law. Individual employment agreements can be terminated by mutual consent, with notice or, in exceptional cases, without notice. Termination for convenience is not possible, neither it is possible to deprive employees of the protection provided by law. Special provisions apply to the termination of fixed-term employment agreements.

[609] Some employees enjoy special protection against dismissal. Dismissal of such employees requires preliminary approval. Depending on the particular case, this approval will have to be obtained from the respective trade union, the Labour Inspectorate and/or an expert medical committee.

[610] The employees enjoying special protection are:

(i) pregnant women;
(ii) mothers of children under the age of three;
(iii) occupational rehabilitees;
(iv) employees suffering from certain diseases, listed in a special ordinance;
(v) employees on permitted leave, during the leave;
(vi) the employees' representatives;
(vii) employees' representatives responsible for health and safety at work;
(viii) members of a special negotiation body[43] or similar;
(ix) employees with executive function in a trade union.

[43] A special negotiating body is a body comprising employee representatives from a number of Member States responsible for negotiating an agreement establishing a European Works Council (see the 1994 EWC Directive (Directive 94/45/EC), Directive 2001/86/EC and Directive 2003/72/EC).

[611] In terms of compensation, upon termination employees are always entitled to a compensation for unused annual paid leave. There are other compensation payments, which vary with the grounds for employment termination. Usually, compensations are between one and three monthly salaries. For example, if the terminating party does not comply with the notice period, it will owe compensation to the other party.

Termination by Mutual Consent

[612] Employment can be terminated by agreement at any time. The agreement must be in writing and there is no need to indicate the exact reason.

[613] The employer can take the initiative and offer termination by mutual consent against compensation. In this case the compensation cannot be less than four times the last monthly gross salary.

Termination by Notice

[614] Employment can be terminated by notice given by either the employer or the employee. The notice must be in writing and duly delivered to the other party. The employer may only serve notice to the employee in specific cases prescribed by the Labour Code. The notice must clearly set out the reason for the termination. The employee may, however, terminate his/her contract without a reason.

[615] A minimum notice period of thirty days and a maximum of three months is provided by law. The notice period must be the same for both the employer and the employee.

Termination by the Employer with Notice

[616] The employer can terminate the employment agreement with notice for the following reasons:

(i) winding-up of the company;
(ii) closure of part of the undertaking or staff cuts;
(iii) decreased volume of work;
(iv) halt of work for more than fifteen days;
(v) the employee lacks the required skills and qualities to effectively perform his/her job;
(vi) the employee lacks the required degree or qualification for the job;
(vii) relocation of the employer to another town or location and a refusal by the employee to follow;
(viii) when the occupied position has to be made available for a former employee reinstated after an unfair dismissal;
(ix) the employee has acquired the right to retire;
(x) the employment has started after the employee has acquired and exercised the right to retire;

(xi) upon change in the job requirements, if the employee no longer meets those requirements;
(xii) the employee objectively cannot perform the job.

Immediate Termination by the Employee Without Notice

[617] The employee can immediately terminate the employment agreement in the following cases:

(i) the employee can no longer perform his/her job due to illness and the employer is not providing another job opportunity that is suitable for the employee;
(ii) the employer delays payment of labour remuneration or compensation under the social security legislation;
(iii) the employer unlawfully changes the working place, the nature of work or the agreed labour remuneration or is not performing obligations that have been agreed in the individual labour agreement or the collective bargaining agreement or other obligations;
(iv) there is a significant adverse change in the working conditions after a transfer of employment;
(v) the employee is appointed a paid elected official or begins scientific research work after winning a contest for this research position;
(vi) the employee continues his/her studies as a full-time student at an educational establishment or enrols in a full-time doctoral programme;
(vii) the employee is working on a fixed-term employment agreement and concludes a labour agreement for an indefinite period of time;
(viii) the employee is working for a temporary work agency and concludes a labour agreement with another employer, which is not a temporary work agency;
(ix) the employee is reinstated to his/her former job, because he/she was unfairly dismissed, and the employee is willing to return to his/her former job;
(x) the employee becomes a government official;
(xi) the employer discontinues its operations;
(xii) the employer has sent the employee on unpaid leave without the employee's consent;
(xiii) the employee has acquired the right to retire due to his/her age and sufficient length of service.

Immediate Termination by the Employer

[618] The employer can immediately terminate the employment agreement in the following cases:

(i) the employee is detained for execution of an effective sentence;

(ii) the employee is deprived of the right to exercise the profession he/she exercising;
(iii) the employee is deprived of his/her academic degree, in the case th employment agreement was concluded based on this degree;
(iv) the employee is deregistered from the register of professional organisa tions of health care specialists;
(v) the employee becomes an occupational rehabilitee and refuses to accept a offer for reassignment to a position suitable for his/her condition;
(vi) the employee is dismissed through disciplinary procedure;
(vii) the employee failed to report a conflict of interests (for employee employed in the state administration);
(viii) the employee has a conflict of interests (for employees in the state admir istration);
(ix) the employee holds public office and a conflict of interest has been estal lished under a special legislation;
(x) an educational specialist has been sentenced for a crime of a general natur (this provision will come into force as of 1 August 2016);
(xi) the employee does not undergo an integrity check under the Counte Corruption and Unlawfully Acquired Assets Forfeiture Act.

Termination Procedure

[619] The Labour Code prescribes a specific procedure that has to be followe upon termination. The employment relationship is usually terminated by an orde from the employer or an authorised person. The order has to be reasoned an well-grounded, especially when the termination is made by the employer unilater ally. Before dismissing an employee on disciplinary grounds, the employer mus ask for and receive the employee's explanations of the case/breach. Otherwise, th court would reverse the dismissal without further investigation. Furthermore, dis ciplinary dismissal has to be imposed within a certain timeframe – at the latest, tw months from discovering the breach of labour discipline but no later than one yea from committing the breach.

[620] Before mass redundancies a special procedure has to be followed. Thi includes, among others, consultations with the employees' representatives and rep resentatives of the trade unions, as well as notification to the Employment Agenc

[621] All employees enjoy the same treatment under Bulgarian law. Generall there is no difference between blue and white collar workers.

Labour Conditions

[622] Labour costs are typically low in Bulgaria, while the workforce is well edu cated and technically skilled. Most young employees speak foreign languages. Th labour costs would depend heavily on the specific sectors, as in sectors where ther is high demand, salaries are typically higher (sometimes two, even three time higher than the salaries in other sectors of the economy).

[623] Collective bargaining agreements do exist, but their number is not high. Under Bulgarian law, the employer can be forced to negotiate such agreement but not to conclude it if the terms are not satisfactory.

[624] Typically, trade unions create difficulties for big companies that employ at least a few hundred employees. However, they are not too powerful. Trade unions traditionally operate in privatised companies and rarely in newly established ones.

Pensions

Types of Pension

[625] Pensions in Bulgaria are governed by law. The Bulgarian pension system has three pillars:

(i) Compulsory state pension scheme – the contributions are mandatory and are distributed among the employer and the employee in a certain ratio, which is prescribed by law.
(ii) Supplementary compulsory pension scheme – this type of scheme is mandatory for working people:
  (a) that are born after 31 December 1959 (universal retirement fund) – the contributions are split between the employer and the employee; or
  (b) that work in less favourable or hazardous working conditions – miners, pilots, some bus drivers, etc. (professional retirement fund) – only the employer makes contributions.

As of 15 August 2015 employees can transfer the accumulated funds from a universal retirement fund to the state operated pension scheme and vice versa. From 1 January 2016, employees can transfer the amount accumulated in a professional retirement fund to the state operated pension scheme, but only once.

(iii) Supplementary voluntary pension scheme – this scheme is voluntary and is based on a contract. The contributions can be made by the employer or by the employee. Sometimes the employer doubles the contribution made by the employee to a certain amount as part of the employee's benefit plan.

Pension Schemes in Light of M&A Transactions

[626] Upon transfer of employment, the new employer generally has to provide the same working conditions as the previous one. This includes pension contributions. This aspect has to be taken into consideration when the transfer includes employees who benefit from a voluntary pension scheme. Such pension schemes are based on contracts and will not transfer automatically. Their assignment should be agreed on separately.

Retention of Key Management and Employees

[627] Certain categories of managers[44] can be hired only under a services agreement. Services agreements differ from the employment agreements and, generally, they provide more freedom for the parties to negotiate the agreement's terms and conditions. The provisions of the Labour Code do not apply to services agreements.

[628] Employees can always leave by giving notice – the maximum notice period that can legally be agreed is three months. This does not apply to managers and the services agreement can be concluded for a fixed term (e.g., four years) or with notice whose period is freely negotiated between the parties.

[629] Contractual provisions are not always able to prevent employees or managers leaving a company. The best approach would be staying in touch with the employees and management and offering them good working conditions – higher salaries, bonus schemes, additional paid leave, etc.

[630] In our practice we have been involved in negotiations with employees for welcome bonuses, retention payments and cashing-in of benefits which, for various reasons, could not be extended or their provision is no longer economically viable for the new employer. There are various options in this regard, whose practicality should be assessed on a case-by-case basis.

Non-compete Undertakings

[631] Non-compete undertakings in both employment and services agreements are valid and enforceable as long as the respective contract is in force. However, there is established case law that post-termination non-compete clauses in labour agreements are null and void. The rationale is that such restrictive covenants limit employees' constitutional rights to freely determine their profession and therefore even tailoring such clauses by adding compensation or a time limit would not make them enforceable. As regards services agreements, the question is more controversial and the case law is inconsistent. Considering the position of the courts as regards employment agreements, the enforceability of post-termination non-compete undertakings in services agreements is also questionable.

[632] Bulgarian law recognises confidentiality undertakings (both in employment and services agreements). They have to be carefully drafted and to specifically define the information that is considered confidential.

[633] Furthermore, courts do recognise non-solicitation undertakings. They are becoming an alternative to the unenforceable non-compete clauses. Bulgarian courts define these as contractual undertakings aimed at prevention of unfair competition. Such covenants could prohibit solicitation of former clients, employees,

---

[44] For example, managing directors of limited liability companies, members of the managing or supervisory board of a joint-stock company.

distributors, etc. Again, they have to be carefully tailored in order to be enforceable.

[634] Non-solicitation undertakings in combination with a well-drafted confidentiality undertaking can provide a decent level of protection of the former employer.

Treatment of Foreign Employees

Foreign Managers and Employees

[635] There are no restrictions on foreign managers under Bulgarian law and many foreign companies have them. There is no specific residency requirement and quite often managers do travel and are responsible for the management of a whole region (e.g., the Balkans, the CEE). Board members or managers working under a services agreement do not need a work permit.

[636] EU, EEA and Swiss nationals can work in Bulgaria without a work permit. Also exempted from the work permit requirement are foreigners with a long-term or permanent Bulgarian residency permit, refugees, members of the family of a Bulgarian, EU, EEA or Swiss national or foreigner with long-term residency permit, etc.

[637] Generally, nationals from third countries need work permits before they can be employed in Bulgaria. Work permits are valid for one year, but their term of validity can be extended. The maximum amount of foreigners working under work permits for a specific Bulgarian company is 20% of the headcount. For small- and medium-sized enterprises, the permitted number is up to 35%.

[638] Bulgarian law also provides an alternative to the work permit for highly qualified employees – the EU Blue Card. Recent legislative changes were aimed at the simplification of the procedure. Among the changes under the amended legislation, before the recruitment of certain specialists employers are no longer obliged to carry out a pre-study of the labour force in Bulgaria in order to prove that there are no Bulgarian citizens, citizens of an EU Member State or a Member State of the EEA residing in Bulgaria who are qualified for the job. The obligation to prove that no local employees can be promptly trained for the company's business needs has also been eliminated.

[639] The EU Single Permit is another alternative to the ordinary work permit.

Work Permits

[640] Generally, the term for issuance of regular work permit is one month, but it can take longer – for example, in the case of missing documents. The fee for a work permit is BGN400 (approximately EUR205).

[641] A temporary residency permit for one year, when such is required, costs BGN500 (approximately EUR255).

Taxation of Foreigners

[642] Foreign employees, both tax residents and non-residents, locally employe by a Bulgarian employer and working in Bulgaria, are taxable in Bulgaria fro their first day of work. The Bulgarian employer will have to put them on the payro and pay the relevant Bulgarian social security contributions and income tax.

[643] As regards taxation and social security contributions of managers, th regime is the same. If the manager works under a service agreement in Bulgari he/she has to pay taxes and make social contributions in Bulgaria. There might b some exceptions – for example when managers travel and work in more than on Member State.

[644] In both cases income tax is fixed at a flat rate of 10%, but the social contri butions are different. Directors working on a service contract are deemed sel employed and are responsible for payment of some of the contributions. In th case of an employment contract, the employer pays both its own and the contribu tions on behalf of the employee.

[645] Apart from that, according to Bulgarian tax legislation, an individual with out domicile in Bulgaria becomes taxable in Bulgaria (tax resident) on his/he worldwide income when any of the following conditions are met:

(i) the individual is registered with a permanent address in Bulgaria;
(ii) the individual is physically present in Bulgaria for a period, or period which exceeds, in aggregate, 183 days in any twelve-month period;
(iii) the individual is a national who has been sent abroad by the Bulgaria state, a governmental organisation or a private company; or
(iv) the individual's centre of vital interests (closest personal and/or economi ties) is in Bulgaria.

Managers' Responsibility

[646] Managing directors and board members are responsible for damage cause to the company they manage and represent.

[647] Board members of a JSC are generally jointly and severally liable unless i can be established that a respective member was not at fault. In addition, boar members have to provide security, which is at least three times their monthly salar

[648] Insurance for damage caused by a board member and managers is not com mon practice in Bulgaria.

ACCOUNTING TREATMENT

Accounting Rules

[649] Bulgarian accountancy rules are governed by the Accountancy Act.

[650] Enterprises should prepare their annual financial statements on the basis of the National Accounting Standards or International Financial Reporting Standards (IFRS). Consolidated financial statements of companies that are allowed to trade their shares on a regulated Member State market are prepared on the basis of IFRS only. Enterprises that prepare their annual financial statements on the basis of IFRS may change their applicable basis of accounting and start preparing the annual financial statements on the basis of the National Accounting Standards. Such a transition can occur only once.

[651] As far as the National Accounting Standards are concerned, they implement to large extent the IFRS. However, recent amendments introduced to IFRS have not been respectively adopted in the Bulgarian Accountancy Act.

Reporting Obligations

[652] The financial year in Bulgaria corresponds to the calendar year; therefore, all entities are required to prepare their annual financial statements as at 31 December.

[653] As a general rule, entities are required to prepare non-consolidated annual financial statements, and only where explicitly provided by law – consolidated ones. The Accountancy Act provides for an exception as regards sole traders whose annual turnover is less than BGN200 000 (approximately EUR100 000) – they only need to prepare an annual income statement.

Annual Financial Statements

[654] The mandatory parts of the financial statements are: (i) statement on the financial position; (ii) income statement; (iii) statement of cash flows; (iv) statement of changes of equity and (v) notes of the preparer to the financial statements.

[655] Companies can choose between the nature of expenses method and the cost of sales method for the format for the statement of comprehensive income, thus allowing them to decide which method corresponds better to the needs of their business.

[656] Parent companies should prepare consolidated financial statements in accordance with the rules established in:

(i) the National Accounting Standards – for the enterprises that compile and submit annual financial statements on the basis of the National Accounting Standards;
(ii) IFRS – for the enterprises that compile and submit annual financial statements on the basis of IFRS.

[657] Such consolidated financial statements should be prepared by the parent company regardless of the location of the seats of its subsidiaries.

Filling Formalities

[658] Companies should prepare their annual financial statements by 31 March of the following year.

[659] The annual financial statements of companies and non-profit legal entities registered with the CR and the Registry of Non-Profit Legal Entities, both kept at the Registry Agency, should be filed with the Commercial Registry by 30 June of the following year.

[660] Entities not registered with the Commercial Registry or Registry of Non-Profit Legal Entities should make available their annual financial statements in the financial press or on the internet not later than 30 June of the following year. Free access to the annual financial statements should be guaranteed for a period of no less than three years after the release date.

FUTURE DEVELOPMENTS

[661] Generally, the Bulgarian economy is on an upward path. A number of sizable transactions were completed in 2017 and at the beginning of 2018, and there are more in the pipeline. The main drivers of M&A are the exits of Greek banks from Bulgaria and the consolidation of the banking sector, as well as the appetite of new investors to establish themselves on the market.

[662] We see also potential in the following sectors:

(i) Telecommunications – this is a sector with stable growth of M&A transactions, globally. We expect that there will also be interest in Bulgarian targets in this sector.
(ii) The IT sector – this sector will continue to attract foreign investors. This will be valid especially for companies with high added value or those specialising in the development of niche products or services. Local companies involved in IT outsourcing are also of interest to foreign investors;
(iii) The financial sector – there were recently a number of transactions in the banking sector, but we still see potential for consolidation of the leasing and insurance sub-sector as well as for an increase in the number of transactions relating to larger non-performing loan portfolios;

(iv) The real estate sector – this sector is generating remarkable volumes of investment in the country, and we believe that this trend will continue, especially in retail and office buildings.